the ultimate book for pasta lovers
truly madly pasta

# truly madly pasta

quadrille

**Ursula Ferrigno**     **photography by Peter Cassidy**

To Richard, my rock and roots, for all you do. I love your cooking too.

First published in 2003 by **Quadrille Publishing Limited** Alhambra House, 27–31 Charing Cross Road, London WC2H OLS

**Text** © Ursula Ferrigno 2003, **Photography** © Peter Cassidy 2003 **Concept, edited text, design & layout** © Quadrille Publishing Ltd 2003
The rights of Ursula Ferrigno to be identified as the Author of this Work have been asserted by her in accordance with the Copyright, Design and Patents Act 1988.

ISBN 184400 018 4    Printed and bound by Dai Nippon in Hong Kong

# 1

# le fondamenta
basics

In Italy, hardly a meal is served without pasta and it has also become incredibly popular all over the world. It is, after all, inexpensive, quick to cook, highly nutritious and extremely versatile. The range of dried and fresh pastas readily available from supermarkets and delicatessens today is seemingly endless and, of course, you can combine these with all manner of really tasty sauces

Pasta is an ancient food, and cave drawings in Imperia, northern Italy, suggest that it was there long before Marco Polo reportedly brought it back from China. Pasta is fundamental to Italian life. It is a daily ritual, consumed at every lunch or dinner, even on Christmas day, as part of the first course, *primo piatto*, after the antipasti and before the main course, and never as a whole meal on its own.

Pasta was once a southern speciality, while in the north they favoured rice and polenta, but pasta has somehow united Italy and it is now eaten the length and breadth of the country. Pasta is the soul of Italian life. During the Renaissance, pasta — especially lasagne, ravioli and tortellini — was found only on the tables of the wealthy. In the nineteenth century, though, it came to be viewed as food for the poor, especially in Naples. In the twentieth century, Mussolini went so far as to consider banning it from the Italian army's diet because he thought it made the soldiers lethargic!

From a nutritional angle, pasta is essentially a complex carbohydrate food, but, because it has a low fat content, it isn't high in calories at all (of course, some of the sauces served with it can be). Some varieties of pasta, notably those made with eggs, contain as much as 13 per cent protein, as well as useful vitamins and minerals.

One's imagination can run riot with ingredients for a pasta sauce: you can use vegetables, pulses, cheeses, oils, herbs and spices. I eat pasta daily; it's the only thing I know I will definitely do each day. My grandfather used to say, 'I'm not living if I haven't eaten pasta every day'.

## Types of pasta

Fresh egg pasta (*pasta fresca all'uovo*) bought vacuum-sealed can be limp and tasteless, but Italian food shops that make pasta on the premises sell something nearer the real thing. Dried pasta (*pasta secca*) is good, especially if made in Italy from durum semolina (*pasta di semola di grano duro secca*), and there are types of dried egg pasta (*pasta all'uovo secca*). However, the ultimate pasta is homemade. Most of the recipes that I have included in this book use the simple pastas, such as spaghetti, tagliatelle and lasagne — those which are most often used at home, *a casa*, in Italy. This saves having many half-used packages of different shapes cluttering your cupboards.

## Making pasta

Pasta should be made from strong flour rich in the gluten that gives pasta its true texture. The wheat is very finely milled to produce '00' grade flour, which is soft and silky. It is available from good delicatessens and Italian delis. Plain flour may be used, but the pasta will be softer.

## Basic egg pasta

**This amount will make enough to serve 12 (it is easier to deal with larger quantities); you can keep the dough in the fridge for several days or freeze what you don't need immediately.**

**makes about 1kg/2¼lb**

**350g/12oz plain flour, preferably Italian 00 (see above)**
350g/12oz semolina flour
**1tsp sea salt**
7 medium eggs (preferably corn-fed and Italian, so the yolks are yellow)
**2 tbsp olive oil**

1 Pile the flours on a work surface, then blend them together, adding the salt, into one large volcano-like pile with crater-like reservoir in the centre.

2 Break the eggs into the reservoir and add the oil. With a fork, slowly break up the eggs and draw in the flour with the other hand to make a paste. When all the flour is mixed in you should have a ball of dough — if it seems too dry, add a little more oil or water, if it seems too damp knead in a little more flour.

3 At first the mixture will be soft and claggy, but knead until it is smooth and silken, and when you press a finger into it the depression bounces back. Wrap in cling film and allow to rest in the refrigerator for about 30 minutes.

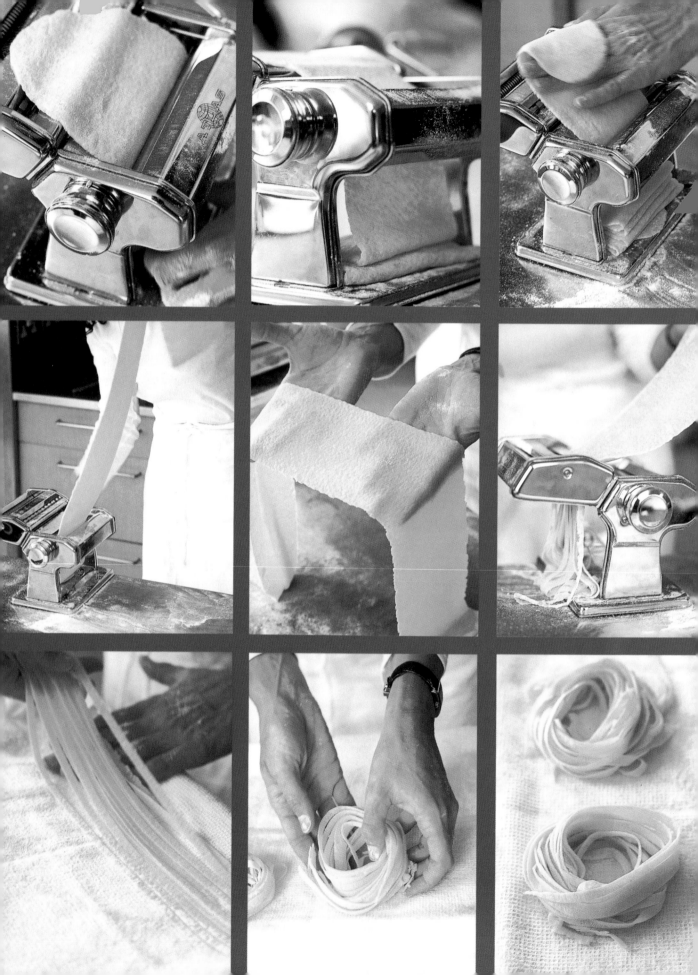

## using a pasta machine

Roll out the rested chilled pasta dough to a long thinnish oval that will just fit into the width of the pasta machine. Starting with the machine rollers set at their widest possible setting, pass the dough through the machine several times.

Change the machine rollers to the next widest setting and repeat the process. Continue down the settings in this way. By the time you have passed the dough several times through the setting one up from the narrowest (I never use the narrowest setting as I find it produces pasta that is so fine that it is too difficult to handle), the pasta should be ready for shaping. It should be thin enough for you to be able to make out your fingers through the sheet as shown.

For things like ravioli and lasagne you can use these pasta sheets just as they are, trimming them to the required shape. To make pasta noodles, however, pass the dough through the selected cutters to produce the shape required. Leave to dry in lengths for 5–7 minutes (otherwise the pasta will stick to itself), then wind handfuls of the lengths of pasta into nests, as shown, and leave them to dry again briefly before cooking.

**For pasta nero** (squid ink pasta): simply add a 4g sachet of squid ink with the eggs and oil. Sachets of squid ink can be found in good fishmongers and Italian delis.

**For paste verde or pasta con spinaci** (spinach pasta): replace 2 of the eggs with 500g/1lb 2oz spinach cooked in a tightly closed pan (just in the water clinging to it after washing) for a few minutes until tender and then allowed to cool. You need to remove as much moisture from it as possible (squeeze it between 2 matching plates).

# Matching sauces to pasta shapes

Pasta is made in hundreds of different shapes, each one with a different ability to cling to the all-important sauce. A simple rule-of-thumb is that hollow or twisted shapes take chunky sauces and that the flatter the pasta, the richer the sauce. Thin and long pasta suits an oily, more liquid sauce; more complicated shapes will have holes and curves in which a thicker sauce can nestle and cling. In fact, new pastas designed to enhance the 'cling' effect are introduced almost as regularly as the new, ever-more-clingy fashions modelled on Milan's catwalks.

Heavy sauces with large chunks of meat are unlikely to go well with thin spaghettini or tagliolini, simply because the chunks will slide off, so these sauces are always served with wide pasta such as pappardelle, maccheroni and tagliatelle or with short tubular shapes such as penne, fusilli, conchiglie and rigatoni.

In the south of Italy, olive oil is used for cooking rather than butter, so there sauces tend to be made with olive oil and they are usually served with dried plain durum wheat pasta (*pasta di semola grano duro*), such as spaghetti and vermicelli. These long thin shapes are traditionally served with tomato and seafood sauces, most of which are made with olive oil, and with light vegetable sauces. Spaghetti and vermicelli are also ideal vehicles for minimalist sauces like Aglio e Olio from Rome (page 34). Grated cheese is not normally used in these sauces, nor is it sprinkled over them.

In the north, butter and cream are used in sauces and, not surprisingly, these go well with the egg pasta that is made there, which absorbs butter and cream and makes the sauce cling to it. Butter and cream also go well with tomato sauces when these are served with short shapes especially penne, rigatoni, farfalle and fusilli.

## Cooking pasta

Cook the pasta in rapidly boiling water, bring back to the boil as quickly as possible and keep at a rolling boil until done. Always cook dried pasta in a large pan so that there is plenty of room for the pasta to expand, as it absorbs water as it cooks. Only salt the water when it is boiling; if the salt is put in too early it will disperse around the sides of the pan and water will not be salty enough.

Dried pasta, which is made from durum wheat, is ready when it is *al dente* (literally 'to the tooth'), that is tender but with a central resistance to the bite. You will see that I have repeated this instruction in full in every recipe and for this I make no apology. I watched my esteemed fellow Italian food writer Antonio Carluccio being criticized on a television programme in which members of the public were asked to cook from one of his books. Even though he had carefully explained the phrase '*al dente*' in the introduction to the book, the readers still complained that because they did not know Italian they didn't know quite what to do.

Fresh pasta, which is made from a softer wheat, is never as firm as dried when cooked, but it should still have some resistance. Overcooked pasta of any kind is limp and unpalatable, and an Italian cook would never serve it.

Stuffed pasta shapes require more gentle handling or they may burst open and release their filling into the water. Accordingly, add them to the boiling water, bring it back to the boil as quickly as possible, then reduce the heat and poach the pasta shapes at a gentle simmer, stirring them gently during cooking.

When cooking spaghetti and other long dried pasta, you need to coil the pasta into the boiling water as it softens. Take a handful at a time and dip it in the boiling water so that it touches the bottom of the pan. As the spaghetti strands soften, coil them round using a wooden spoon or fork until they are all submerged.

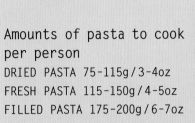

Amounts of pasta to cook
per person
DRIED PASTA 75-115g/3-4oz
FRESH PASTA 115-150g/4-5oz
FILLED PASTA 175-200g/6-7oz

Cooking ready-made fresh pasta is generally much quicker and can be as rapid as 4-5 minutes, although this will depend on the shape and size, e.g. lasagne. Homemade tagliatelle can actually cook in as little as 30 seconds.

I actually cook my pasta in bottled Italian water whenever possible; it's terribly extravagant but the pasta tastes amazing.

## Serving pasta

The most important thing of all is to have your family and friends waiting at the table for the pasta, not the other way around. Pasta waits for no one. Cook it, dress it and serve it at once. In Italy, it is served in a deep plate, which prevents the sauce from splashing and helps to keep the pasta warm. The pasta is never served in a huge mound. Recipes vary in the way they combine sauce and pasta. The majority add the sauce to the pasta. There are no hard-and-fast rules, but always have warmed bowls ready.

Freshly grated Parmesan cheese, the best being Parmigiano Reggiano, is sprinkled on most pasta dishes, enhancing the nutritional benefits with its added protein and calcium. It is not, however, added to most mushroom or fish and shellfish pasta dishes.

## Eating Pasta

Do it with a fork only please, using it to lift the pasta and sauce together. Make a small space at the side of your plate and twist. The trick is to twizzle only a small amount around the fork at a time. *Buon appetito!*

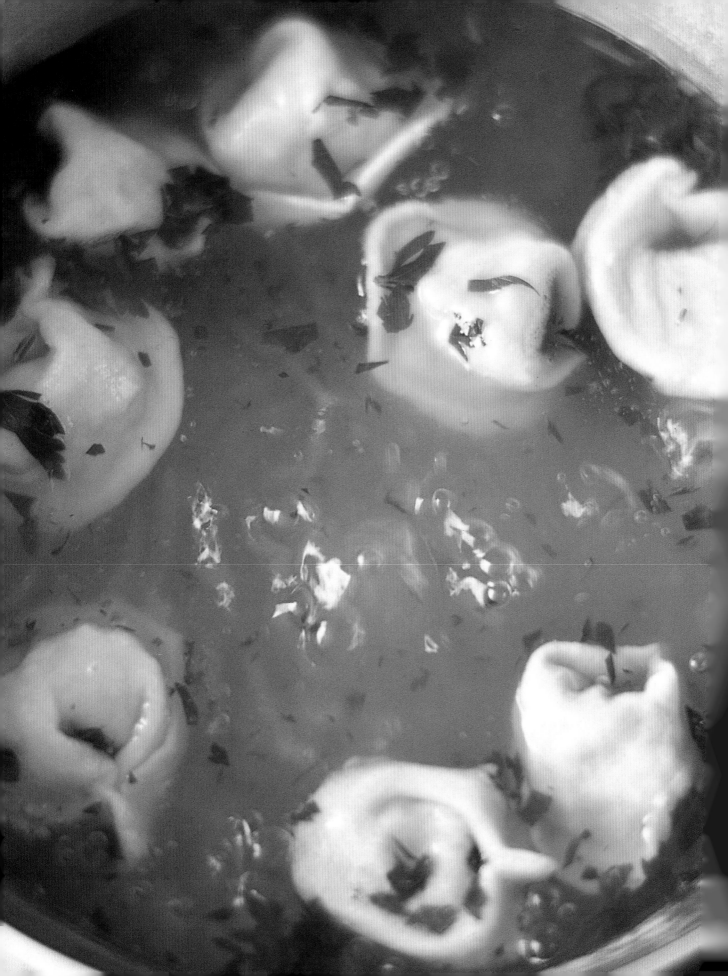

# zuppe e minestre

soups & stocks

Pasta in soup is very much a part of traditional Italian home cooking, although its role in this respect is rather overlooked abroad. Served as a *primo piatto* instead of an ordinary pasta dish, it is seen as highly digestible energy-giving food for fuel. Usually with lots of added vegetables and/or pulses, it makes the ultimate comfort food in winter. Importantly, the Italians don't see soups as a repository for leftovers, but use the best and freshest of ingredients and put some energy into making the tastiest of stocks on which to base their pasta *in brodo*.

# Minestrone alla Genovese Genoese Minestrone (with Pesto) serves 4–6

In Genoa they often make minestrone like this, with some of their local pesto stirred into the soup towards the end of cooking. Maltagliati, literally meaning 'badly cut', are pasta from Emilia-Romagna made by cutting sheets of pasta into irregular shapes; small pieces are often used in soup.

1 onion

2 celery stalks

2 medium carrots

3 tbsp olive oil

150g/5oz French beans, cut into 5cm/2in pieces

1 courgette, thinly sliced

1 potato, cut into 1cm/½in cubes

¼ Savoy cabbage, shredded

200g/7oz cooked or rinsed canned cannellini beans

2 Italian plum tomatoes, chopped

1. 2 litres/2 pints vegetable stock

sea salt and freshly ground black pepper

90g/3¼oz dried vermicelli or maltagliati (see above)

**FOR THE PESTO**

1 garlic clove

2 tsp pine nuts

2 tbsp extra-virgin olive oil

1 tbsp freshly grated Parmesan cheese

1 tbsp freshly grated Pecorino cheese

20 basil leaves

1 Chop the onion, celery and carrot finely. Heat the oil in a large saucepan, add the chopped vegetables and cook over a low heat, stirring frequently for 5–7 minutes.

2 Mix in the French beans, courgette, potato and cabbage. Stir-fry over a medium heat for about 3 minutes. Add the cannellini beans and tomatoes, and stir-fry for 2–3 minutes.

3 Pour in the stock with salt and pepper to taste. Bring to the boil, stir well, cover and simmer, stirring occasionally, until all the vegetables are tender, about 40 minutes.

4 Meanwhile, make the pesto using a pestle and mortar: starting by pounding the garlic with the pine nuts, then add the oil, cheeses and basil in that order until you have a thick sauce. You can use a food processor, but the flavour is then not as pungent.

5 Break the pasta into small pieces and add to the soup. Simmer, stirring frequently, for 5 minutes. Add the pesto sauce and stir it in well, then simmer for 2–3 minutes more or until the pasta is al dente, i.e. tender but still firm to the bite.

6 Taste and adjust the seasoning if necessary. Serve the minestrone in warmed bowls.

## Variation

You could dress the soup with any of the other versions of pesto in the book, such as Roasted Red Pepper Pesto or Wild Rocket Pesto (see pages 111–12).

# Minestrone di Pasta e Ceci Minestrone with Pasta and Chickpeas   serves 4–6

**Typical of the Molise region, this recipe delivers double carbohydrates for long-term energy. The flavour of rosemary works well with almost all types of pulse.**

4 tbsp olive oil

1 onion, finely chopped

2 carrots, finely chopped

2 celery stalks, finely chopped

400g / 14oz cooked chickpeas

200g / 7oz cooked or rinsed canned cannellini beans

150ml / ¼ pint passata

2 fresh rosemary sprigs

sea salt and freshly ground black pepper

200g / 7oz conchiglie

freshly grated Parmesan cheese, to serve

**FOR THE VEGETABLE STOCK**

1 onion, halved

7 cloves

3 celery stalks

2 carrots

2–3 leeks

handful of potato peelings, well cleaned

2 garlic cloves, halved

a little olive oil

3 fresh bay leaves, torn

handful of flat-leaf parsley with stalks

1 First make the vegetable stock: stud the onion halves with the cloves and coarsely chop the other vegetables. Heat the oil in a large heavy-based saucepan and gently sauté all these vegetables until lightly coloured. Add the remaining ingredients with cold water to cover and very lightly season. Bring to the boil, skim well, lower the heat and simmer gently for 25–35 minutes.

2 Towards the end of this time, heat the oil in a large saucepan, add the finely chopped vegetables and cook over a low heat, stirring frequently, for 5–7 minutes.

3 Add the chickpeas and cannellini beans, stir well to mix, then cook for 5 minutes. Stir in the passata and 125ml / 4fl oz water, and cook, stirring, for 2–3 minutes.

4 Add 600ml / 1 pint of the sieved stock, 1 of the rosemary sprigs and salt and pepper to taste. Bring to the boil, cover then simmer gently, stirring occasionally, for 1 hour.

5 Add another 1 litre / 1¾ pint of sieved stock and the pasta, and bring to the boil, stirring. Lower the heat and simmer, stirring frequently, until the pasta is al dente, i.e. tender but still firm to the bite, 7–8 minutes. Taste and adjust the seasoning.

6 Remove the rosemary sprig and serve the soup hot in warmed bowls, topped with grated Parmesan and fresh rosemary leaves.

## Variation
Instead of the chickpeas, you could use a variety of other pulses, such as cannellini, borlotti or even butter beans.

# Minestra con Pasta e Verdure Arrostite Minestrone with Pasta and Roasted Vegetables serves 4–6

This is a classic Italian family dish with a twist. Every Italian home will have its own version of the *minestra*, which means nothing more than 'mixture'. As there is no real fixed format, you can use whatever you like, whatever you have to hand and, preferably, whatever is at its best.

200g/7oz fresh ripe tomatoes (plum or vine-ripened)
3 tbsp olive oil
1 onion
2 celery stalks
2 medium carrots
1 courgette, thinly sliced
1 potato cut into 1cm/½ in cubes
150g/5oz French beans, cut into 5cm/2in pieces
¼ Savoy cabbage shredded
3 garlic cloves, finely chopped
3 fresh bay leaves
200g/7oz cooked cannellini beans
1.2 litres/2 pints vegetable stock
sea salt and freshly ground black pepper
90g/3¼oz dried vermicelli or maltagliati (see page 18)
freshly grated Parmesan cheese, to serve

1 Preheat the oven to 200°C/400°F/Gas 6.

2 Remove their stems and place the tomatoes in a roasting tin. Drizzle with a little of the olive oil and roast in the oven for 20–30 minutes or so, depending on their size, until they begin to colour and the skins split. Remove from the oven and allow to cool slightly before peeling off the skins and chopping roughly.

3 Chop the onion, celery and carrots into dice. Drizzle over a little olive oil and mix to coat the vegetables lightly. Season, spread in a single layer on an oven tray and roast for 5–10 minutes. Add the courgette and potato and return to the oven for another 5–10 minutes, until the onions and carrots are starting to caramelize and the courgettes and potatoes are lightly browned.

4 Heat the last of the oil in a large saucepan and stir-fry the French beans, cabbage and garlic for 3 minutes. Add the bay leaves, cannellini beans and all the roasted vegetables, then pour in the stock with salt and pepper to taste. Bring to the boil, stir well, cover and simmer for 30 minutes or so, until the vegetables are tender, stirring occasionally.

5 Break the pasta into small pieces and add to the soup. Simmer, stirring frequently, for 6–8 minutes or until the pasta is al dente, i.e. just tender but still firm to the bite. Taste and adjust the seasoning if necessary. Serve in warm bowls, sprinkled with Parmesan.

## minestrone primavera (with spring vegetables)

Roast the onion, celery and carrots to develop a good base flavour, then stir-fry 150g/5oz each podded fresh peas, french beans, chopped plum tomatoes and sliced courgettes with the garlic (omit the cabbage). Finish as for the basic recipe, with or without the beans.

## minestrone di fagioli (with beans)

Make the soup base with the onion, celery and carrots. Omit all the other vegetables but add 200g/7oz cooked or rinsed canned borlotti beans and chickpeas with the cannellini. Finish with lots of chopped parsley.

## minestrone inverno (with autumn/winter vegetables)

Make the soup base with the onion, celery and carrots. Use half a Savoy cabbage and 150g/5oz each chopped turnip, winter squash, potatoes and carrots instead of the French beans and courgette (you can roast the winter vegetables if you like). You can add rinsed cannellini or borlotti beans, according to preference.

minestrone estate (with summer vegetables,
red and green peppers) **Roast 3 peppers (2 red
and 1 green) with the tomatoes. Peel off the blackened skin
and chop as with the tomatoes (reserve any juices and add to
the soup). Add other summer vegetables as you wish, making
sure you include a courgette (2 would be even better), and
proceed as with the basic recipe.**

# Millescosedde Pasta, Bean & Vegetable Soup   serves 4–6

**The name of this Calabrian speciality comes from the Italian word *millescose*, meaning 'a thousand things'. Literally anything edible can go in this soup. In Calabria they include a bean called *cicerchia*, which can be found only in this region; here I use cannellini beans and chickpeas.**

**85g/3oz brown lentils**

3 fresh bay leaves

**15g/$\frac{1}{2}$oz dried mushrooms**

175ml/6fl oz warm water

**4 tbsp olive oil**

I carrot, diced

**I celery stalk, diced**

I onion, finely chopped

**I garlic clove, finely chopped**

handful of chopped fresh flat-leaf parsley

**pinch of chilli flakes (optional)**

1.5 litres/2$\frac{1}{4}$ pints vegetable stock

**150g/5oz cooked cannellini beans**

150g/5oz cooked chickpeas

**sea salt and freshly ground black pepper**

115g/4oz dried small pasta shapes

**freshly grated Pecorino cheese, to serve**

chopped flat-leaf parsley, to garnish

1 Put the lentils in a medium-sized pan with the bay leaves. Add 450ml/$\frac{3}{4}$ pint water and bring to the boil over a high heat. Lower the heat to a gentle simmer and cook, stirring occasionally, for 15–20 minutes, or until the lentils are just tender.

2 Meanwhile, soak the dried mushrooms in the warm water for 15–20 minutes.

3 Tip the cooked lentils into a sieve to drain, then rinse under cold running water. Drain the soaked mushrooms and reserve the soaking liquid. Finely chop the mushrooms and set aside.

4 Heat the oil in a large saucepan and add the carrot, celery, onion, garlic, parsley and chillies if using. Cook over a low heat, stirring constantly, for 5–7 minutes. Add the stock, then the mushrooms and their soaking liquid. Bring to the boil and add the beans, chickpeas and lentils, with salt and pepper to taste. Cover and simmer gently for 20 minutes.

5 Add the pasta and bring the soup back to the boil, stirring frequently, until the pasta is al dente, i.e. tender but still firm to the bite, 7–8 minutes.

6 Adjust the seasoning, then serve hot in soup bowls, with grated Pecorino and chopped parsley.

## Variations
You could make this soup with any seasonal vegetables and a variety of other pulses, including borlotti and broad beans.

## Zuppa di Lenticchie e Pastina Lentil and Pasta Soup serves 4-6

175g / 6oz brown lentils

3 garlic cloves

3 tbsp olive oil

25g / 1oz butter

1 onion, finely chopped

2 celery stalks, finely chopped

2 tbsp sun-dried tomato paste

1. 2 litres / 2 pints vegetable stock

a few fresh marjoram leaves

a few fresh basil leaves

leaves from 1 fresh thyme sprig

sea salt and freshly ground black pepper

50g / 2oz dried small pasta shapes

herb leaves, to garnish

1 Put the lentils in a large pan. Add a smashed garlic clove, pour in 1 litre/ 1¾ pints water and bring to the boil. Lower heat to a gentle simmer and cook, stirring occasionally, for 20 minutes or until the lentils are just tender. Tip the lentils into a sieve, remove the garlic and set it aside. Rinse the lentils under cold running water, then leave them to drain.

2 Heat 2 tablespoons of the oil with half of the butter in a large saucepan. Add the onion and celery, and cook over a low heat, stirring frequently for 5–7 minutes until softened. Crush the remaining garlic, then peel and add to the vegetables with the remaining oil, the tomato paste and the lentils. Stir, then add the stock, the fresh herbs and salt and pepper to taste. Bring to the boil, stirring, and simmer for 30 minutes, stirring occasionally.

3 Add the pasta and bring back to the boil, stirring. Simmer, stirring frequently, until the pasta is al dente, i.e. tender but still firm to the bite, 7–8 minutes. Add the remaining butter, taste and adjust the seasoning. Serve hot in warm bowls, sprinkled with the herb leaves.

## Zuppa Casalinga Farmhouse Soup serves 4-6

2 tbsp olive oil

1 onion, roughly chopped

3 carrots

175–200g / 6–7oz turnips

175g / 6oz swede

400g / 14oz can of chopped tomatoes

1 tbsp tomato purée

handful of mixed fresh herbs, such as rosemary, thyme and parsley

1 tsp dried oregano

sea salt and freshly ground black pepper

1. 5 litres / 2½ pints vegetable stock (page 19) or water

50g / 2oz dried small macaroni

400g / 14oz cooked or rinsed canned borlotti or cannellini beans

handful of parsley, to garnish

freshly grated Parmesan, to serve

1 Heat the oil in a large saucepan, add the onion and cook over a low heat for about 5 minutes until softened.

2 Cut all the fresh vegetables into large chunks and add them with the canned tomatoes, tomato purée, fresh herbs and dried oregano with salt and pepper to taste. Pour in the stock or water and bring to the boil. Stir well, cover, lower the heat and simmer for 30 minutes, stirring occasionally.

3 Add the pasta and bring to the boil, stirring. Lower the heat and simmer, uncovered and stirring frequently, until the pasta is just al dente, i.e. tender but still firm to the bite, about 5 minutes.

4 Stir in the beans and heat through for 2–3 minutes, then remove from the heat and stir in the parsley. Taste the soup and adjust the seasoning.

5 Serve hot in warmed soup bowls, with grated Parmesan handed round separately.

# Pesce con Fregula Sardinian Fish Stew serves 4–6

This Sardinian speciality is a cross between a soup and a stew. Fregula is actually a type of couscous, but small soup pasta can also be used. Serve with some Italian country bread to mop up the delicious broth.

**5 tbsp olive oil**

**4 garlic cloves, finely chopped**

**½ small fresh red chilli, deseeded and finely chopped**

**1 large handful of flat-leaf parsley, roughly chopped**

**1 red snapper, about 450g/1lb, cleaned and with head and tail removed**

**1 red or grey mullet, about 500g/1¼lb, cleaned and with head and tail removed**

**350g–450g/12oz–1lb thick cod fillet**

**400g/14oz can of chopped Italian plum tomatoes**

**sea salt and freshly ground black pepper**

**175g/6oz dried fregula (see above) or pastina or pantaletti**

1 Heat 2 tablespoons of the olive oil in a large flameproof casserole. Add the chopped garlic and chilli with about half the chopped parsley. Fry over a medium heat, stirring occasionally, for about 5 minutes, taking care not to brown the garlic.

2 Cut all of the fish into large chunks, leaving the skin and bones in place in the case of the snapper and mullet, adding the pieces to the casserole as you cut them. Sprinkle with a further 2 tablespoons of the olive oil and fry for a few minutes more.

3 Add the tomatoes, then fill the empty can with water and pour this into the pan. Bring to the boil. Stir in salt and pepper to taste, lower the heat and cook for 10 minutes, stirring occasionally.

4 Add the fregula or pasta and simmer for 5 minutes, then add 250ml/9fl oz of water and the remaining oil. Simmer for 15 minutes.

5 If the soup becomes too thick, add more water. Taste and adjust the seasoning. Serve hot in warm bowls, sprinkled with the remaining parsley.

Consiglio  Any number of different fish can be included in this delicious stew; you can replace the snapper with a white fish like haddock, and I have made it with plaice and sea bass to great effect. Remove all bones if you prefer.

# Zuppa di Vongole e Pastina Clam and Pasta Soup  serves 4–6

**Subtly sweet and spicy, this soup is substantial enough to be served on its own for lunch or supper. A crusty loaf is my favourite accompaniment.**

225g/8oz clams
a little plain flour
2 tbsp olive oil
I onion, finely chopped
leaves from I fresh thyme sprig, plus extra for garnish
2 garlic cloves, crushed
5–6 fresh basil leaves, torn, plus extra for garnish
½ tsp chilli flakes
I litre/1¾ pints fish stock
350ml/12fl oz passata
I tsp sugar
sea salt and freshly ground black pepper
85g/3oz fresh peas
65g/2¼oz dried small pasta

1 Keep the clams submerged in water with a little added plain flour (this helps plump them up and purge them of any dirt). Discard any clams that remain open when tapped.

2 Heat the oil in a large saucepan, add the onion and cook gently for about 5 minutes, until softened but not coloured. Add the thyme, then stir in the garlic, basil, chilli, stock, passata and sugar, with salt and pepper to taste. Bring to the boil, then lower the heat and simmer gently, stirring occasionally, for 15 minutes. Add the peas and cook for a further 5 minutes.

3 Add the pasta and bring to the boil, stirring. Lower the heat and simmer, stirring frequently, until the pasta is only just al dente, i.e. tender but still firm to the bite, about 5 minutes.

4 Turn the heat down to low, add the clams and cook for 5–7 minutes until the clams open (discard any that stubbornly refuse to). Adjust the seasoning.

5 Serve hot, garnished with extra basil and thyme.

## Variation
If pressed, you can make a fairly reputable version of this dish with canned clams – but look for an Italian brand and rinse them well! Flavourful jarred clams in brine are also now widely available in better supermarkets.

# Pastina in Brodo Pasta in Meat Broth   serves 4

**about 450g/1lb meat bones (any type, or a mixture, will do — ask your butcher)**

**3 fresh bay leaves**

**sea salt and freshly ground black pepper**

**2 ripe tomatoes**

**65g/2¼oz small soup pasta, such as farfalline (little farfalle, see page 45)**

**1 tbsp extra-virgin olive oil**

**25g/1oz freshly grated Parmesan cheese**

**handful of flat-leaf parsley, finely chopped**

1 Preheat the oven to 200°C/400°F/Gas 6. Put the bones in a large roasting tin and roast in the preheated oven for 25 minutes, until well coloured.

2 Put the browned bones in a large pan and cover with water. Add the bay leaves and season with salt. Bring to the boil, skim well and then simmer gently for 40 minutes, skimming from time to time if necessary. Strain.

3 Meanwhile, put the tomatoes in a bowl, cover with boiling water for about 40 seconds then plunge them into cold water. Using a sharp knife, peel off the skins and finely chop the flesh, discarding the seeds.

4 Add the tomatoes to the strained stock and cook for 2–3 minutes more.

5 Stir in the pasta and cook for 3–5 minutes until it is just tender. Season with salt and pepper to taste and stir in the olive oil.

6 Serve sprinkled with Parmesan cheese and parsley.

# Pasta in Brodo con Piselli e Fegatini Pasta Soup with Peas and Chicken Livers   serves 4–6

**115g/4oz fresh chicken livers**

**1 tbsp olive oil**

**knob of unsalted butter**

**4 garlic cloves, crushed**

**3 sprigs of parsley**

**3 sprigs of marjoram**

**3 sprigs of sage**

**leaves from a sprig of fresh thyme**

**sea salt and freshly ground black pepper**

**1–2 tbsp dry white wine**

**1. 2 litres/2 pints chicken stock**

**4 medium potatoes, peeled and cubed**

**225g/8oz shelled fresh peas, shelled**

**50g/2oz dried pasta shapes, such as farfalle (see page 45)**

**handful of basil**

1 Trim the chicken livers and cut into small pieces (this is best done with scissors). Chop the herbs.

2 Heat the oil and butter in a frying pan, add the garlic and herbs, with salt and pepper to taste, and fry gently for a few minutes. Add the livers, increase the heat to high and stir-fry for a few minutes until they change colour and become dry. Pour the wine over and cook until it evaporates, then remove from the heat, taste and adjust the seasoning.

3 Put the chicken stock in a large saucepan with some seasoning and bring to the boil. Add the potatoes and the peas, and simmer for 5 minutes, then add the pasta. Bring the soup back to the boil, stirring, and allow to simmer, stirring frequently, until the pasta is just al dente, i.e. tender but still firm to the bite, about 5 minutes.

4 Add the fried chicken livers and basil, and warm through, adjust the seasoning and serve hot in warmed bowls.

# 3 all'istante

instant

Pasta is one of the easiest of foods to cook in a hurry. In the 10 minutes or so it takes to cook most dried pastas, there are lots of wonderful tasty sauces that can be made. Some can even be put together in the minutes that fresh pasta needs and a few can literally be made at the table. The secret to enjoying any number of fast pasta dishes is having the right things in your storecupboard, like good oil, canned Italian plum tomatoes, canned cannelini or borlotti beans or chickpeas, and cans of anchovies, tuna and vongole. With a good chunk of Parmesan in the fridge, together with eggs, cream and possibly some bacon or pancetta, and you can conjure up a veritable feast. A couple of fresh herbs, such as parsley, chives and basil, will heighten the magic.

## Spaghetti con Cacio e Pepe Spaghetti with Cheese and Pepper   serves 2

**This Roman dish is the perfect storecupboard stand-by.**

**200g / 7oz spaghetti**
sea salt
**little knob of unsalted butter**
50g / 2oz freshly grated Parmesan cheese
**½ tsp freshly ground black pepper**

1 Cook the spaghetti in a large saucepan of boiling salted water for about 10 minutes until al dente, i.e. just tender but still firm to the bite.

2 Drain the pasta and add the butter, cheese and pepper. Stir well and serve straight away. It couldn't be simpler!

## Pasta all'Aglio e Olio Pasta with Garlic and Oil   serves 2

**Versions of this simple classic pop up all over Italy, and they are almost always more than acceptable. It is one of those dishes that most Italian families enjoy at least once a week, often as supper on Monday evenings.**

**200g / 7oz spaghetti**
sea salt
**2 garlic cloves, crushed**
½ small fresh red chilli, deseeded and finely chopped, or 1 small dried pepper (peperoncino), crushed
**4–5 tbsp fruity or lemony extra-virgin olive oil**
handful of flat-leaf parsley, finely chopped

1 Cook the pasta in boiling salted water for about 10 minutes until al dente, i.e. just tender but still firm to the bite.

2 Meanwhile, beat the garlic, chilli and a pinch of salt into the olive oil.

3 When the pasta is cooked, drain and quickly dress with the oil mixture. Serve sprinkled generously with the parsley.

### Variation
You can ring the changes on this considerably by adding some more pungent flavourings, such as finely grated lemon zest, chopped capers, stoned olives or rinsed anchovies.

### Consiglio   To mask the smell of garlic on the breath, try a glass of milk, a handful of parsley, an apple, a strong espresso coffee or a measure of Campari.

# Spaghetti con Pomodori Freschi Spaghetti with Fresh Tomato Sauce   serves 2

**To ensure maximum flavour, use the reddest, ripest tomatoes you can find.**

**200g / 7oz spaghetti**
sea salt and freshly ground black pepper
**6 ripe tomatoes**
**2 garlic cloves, crushed**
**3 tbsp olive oil**
50g / 2oz freshly grated Parmesan cheese, plus extra to serve
**handful of torn fresh basil leaves**

1 Cook the spaghetti in a large saucepan of boiling salted water for about 10 minutes until just al dente, i.e. tender but still firm to the bite.

2 Meanwhile, chop the tomatoes and put in a bowl with the garlic, olive oil, Parmesan cheese, basil, salt and pepper. Mix together.

3 Drain the cooked pasta and toss with the sauce. Serve immediately with extra grated cheese if wished.

# Pasta alla Crudaiola Pasta with Raw Tomato Sauce   serves 4

**This is a wonderfully simple uncooked tomato sauce (*crudaiola* means 'raw') that goes well with many different kinds of pasta, both longs strands and short shapes. However, I prefer it with long pasta, especially bucatini or spaghetti. It is always made in summer, when the plum tomatoes have ripened on the vine in the sun and have their fullest flavour.**

**350g / 12oz pasta of your choice**
500g / 1¼lb ripe Italian plum tomatoes
**1 large handful of fresh basil leaves**
5 tbsp extra-virgin olive oil
**115g / 4oz ricotta salata (firm ricotta, see Consiglio), diced**
1 garlic clove, crushed
**sea salt and freshly ground black pepper**
coarsely shaved Pecorino cheese, to serve

1 Cook the pasta in a pan of salted boiling water until al dente, i.e. just tender but still firm to the bite.

2 Meanwhile, roughly chop the plum tomatoes, removing the cores and as many of the seeds as you can. Tear the basil leaves into shreds with your fingers.

3 Put all the ingredients except the Pecorino in a bowl with salt and pepper to taste and stir well. (If you are not in a hurry, it is a good idea at this point to cover the bowl and leave at room temperature for 1–2 hours, to let the flavours mingle. Obviously you wouldn't cook the pasta until then either.)

4 Taste the sauce and adjust the seasoning if necessary, then toss it with the hot cooked pasta. Serve immediately, with the Pecorino handed round separately.

Consiglio **Ricotta salata is a salted and dried version of ricotta. Firmer than traditional soft white ricotta, it can easily be diced, crumbled or grated. Young soft Pecorino can be used in its place.**

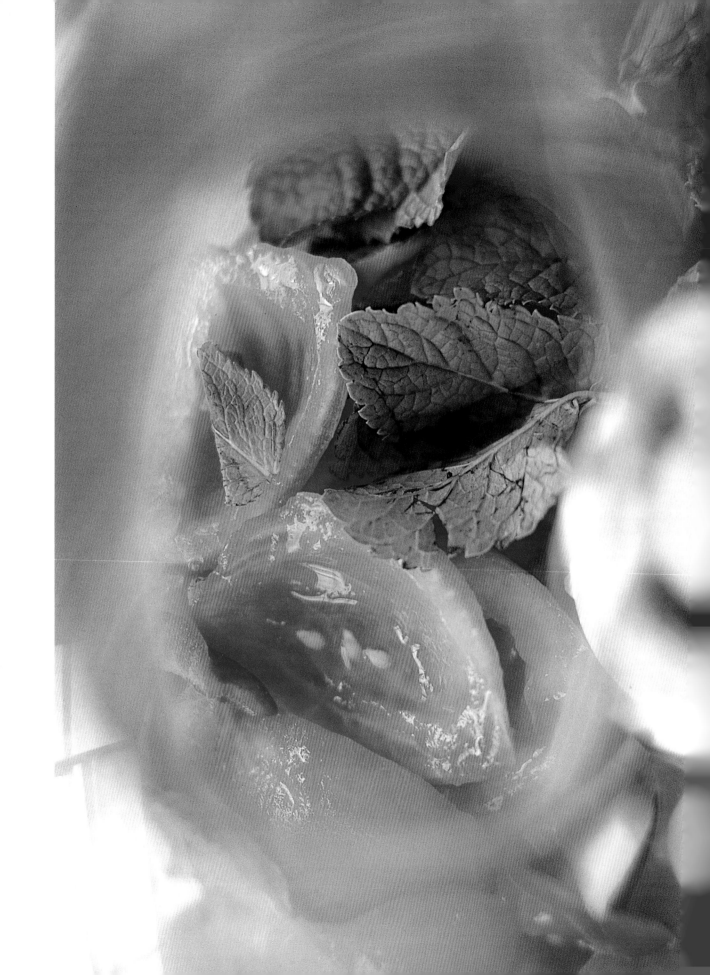

# Spaghetti al Mortaio Spaghetti with Puréed Tomatoes, Red Pepper, Basil and Mint   serves 4

*'Al mortaio'* actually means 'in a mortar', and refers to the fact that here the sauce is a purée. I make it in a blender, but originally it would have been pounded with a pestle in a mortar. This is one of those dishes in which the sauce's flavour is very much a function of the quality of the olive oil used.

375g/13oz spaghetti

sea salt and freshly ground black pepper

600g/1lb 5oz ripe tomatoes

½ garlic clove

1 sweet red pepper, deseeded and sliced

handful of fresh mint leaves

3 tbsp fruity extra-virgin olive oil, ideally finest estate-bottled

handful of fresh basil leaves

50g/2oz freshly grated Parmesan cheese

1 Cook the spaghetti in a large saucepan of boiling salted water until just al dente, i.e. tender but still firm to the bite.

2 Meanwhile, scald the tomatoes with boiling water, then skin them. Cut them in half and remove the seeds.

3 Place the tomatoes in a food processor with salt and pepper to taste, the garlic, sliced red pepper and mint. Blend well until the sauce becomes smooth and uniform. Adjust the seasoning if necessary.

4 Drain the spaghetti well and return to the pan. Add the fruity extra-virgin oil, the puréed sauce and the basil, and mix well. Serve with the cheese.

# Penne con Fave e Ricotta Penne with Broad Beans and Ricotta   serves 4

This is a springtime treat in southern Italy, while young fresh broad beans are in abundance. Don't try it with cooked dried broad beans. Very young beans are even eaten raw with Pecorino. Most common in Liguria and Campania, penne are tube-shaped pasta cut at an angle to make them look like quills. Penne rigate, with ribbing on the outside of the quills, are among the best sauce retainers.

150g/5oz shelled broad beans
200g/7oz penne
sea salt and freshly ground black pepper
1 tbsp olive oil
1 garlic clove, crushed
25g/1oz freshly grated Pecorino cheese
50g/2oz ricotta
about 2 tbsp extra-virgin olive oil
fresh marjoram leaves, to garnish

1 Steam the broad beans for 6 minutes until tender.

2 Meanwhile, cook the penne in a large saucepan of boiling salted water for 10 minutes until just al dente, i.e. tender but still firm to the bite.

3 Heat the olive oil in a saucepan and fry the garlic until lightly browned.

4 Drain the pasta and add to the pan with the broad beans, Pecorino and ricotta, extra-virgin olive oil, and some salt and pepper. Toss well together.

5 Serve garnished with marjoram leaves.

## Fettuccine all'Alfredo Alfredo's Fettuccine (with cream and cheese)    serves 4

This simple recipe was invented in the 1920s by a Roman restaurateur called **Alfredo**, who became famous for serving it with a golden fork and spoon. You can use tagliatelle, which is what the northern Italians call fettuccine, although tagliatelle strips are slightly narrower.

**50g/2oz unsalted butter**
200ml/7fl oz double cream
**50g/2oz freshly grated Parmesan cheese, plus extra to serve**
sea salt and freshly ground black pepper
**350g/12oz fresh fettuccine or tagliatelle**

1 Melt the butter in a large saucepan, add the cream and bring to just below the boil. Simmer for 5 minutes, stirring, then add the Parmesan, with salt and pepper to taste, and turn off the heat under the pan.

2 Bring a large saucepan of salted water to the boil. Drop in the pasta all at once and quickly bring back to the boil, stirring occasionally. Cook until al dente, 2–3 minutes. Drain well.

3 Turn the heat under the pan of cream to low, add the pasta all at once and toss until it is coated in the sauce. Taste for seasoning. Serve at once with extra cheese if necessary.

## Bucatini con Zucchini Bucatini with Courgettes    serves 4

Long and thin, pale in colour and heavily ridged, Romanesco courgettes give the best results, so do look out for them. Bucatini are the long hollow noodles, like slightly fatter spaghetti but with a hole down the middle to help them cook faster.

**375g/13oz bucatini (see above)**
sea salt and freshly ground black pepper
**150ml/¼ pint olive oil**
450g/1lb small tender courgettes
**115g/4oz Parmesan cheese, freshly grated, plus more to serve if you like**
115g/4oz sweet Provolone cheese, freshly grated, plus more to serve if you like
**50g/2oz unsalted butter, cut into little pieces**
handful of basil leaves, torn
**handful of mint leaves, torn**
1 garlic clove, crushed
**2 tbsp fruity extra-virgin olive oil**

1 Cook the bucatini in a large saucepan of boiling salted water until just al dente, i.e. tender but still firm to the bite.

2 Meanwhile, heat the olive oil in a sauté pan, cut the courgettes into thin slices and fry these, a few at a time, in hot oil until lightly golden. Remove and place in a large bowl.

3 Add the two cheeses, butter, basil, mint and garlic to the bowl, and season with salt and pepper.

4 Drain the cooked pasta thoroughly and mix well with the contents of the bowl.

5 Serve immediately, drizzled with the fruity extra virgin olive oil and with extra cheese if desired.

# Rigatoni con Pignoli e Gorgonzola Rigatoni with Gorgonzola and Pine Nuts    serves 2

This northern dish makes the most of tasty **Gorgonzola. I** prefer it made with sharp **Gorgonzola piccante, but you could try the dolce variety if you prefer a milder cheese flavour. Rigatoni are large pasta tubes which are ribbed on the outside. Their size and shape suit strongly flavoured sauces.**

**65g/2¼oz broccoli florets**
65g/2¼oz cauliflower florets
**200g/7oz rigatoni (see above)**
sea salt and freshly ground black pepper
**45g/1½oz pine nuts**
2 tbsp olive oil
**1 red onion, finely chopped**
1 tsp chopped fresh thyme
**115g/4oz Gorgonzola cheese**

1 Steam the broccoli and cauliflower florets for about 12 minutes, depending on their size, until tender.

2 At the same time, cook the rigatoni in a large saucepan of boiling salted water until just al dente, i.e. tender but still firm to the bite.

3 Meanwhile, toast the pine nuts on a sheet of foil under the grill, turning them frequently.

4 Heat the oil in a saucepan and fry the onion until softened. Add the thyme, salt and pepper.

5 Cut the cheese into cubes and add to the onion, along with the toasted nuts, broccoli and cauliflower.

6 Drain the pasta and toss into the mixture. Adjust the seasoning to taste and serve.

## Variation
You can toast the pine nuts in a dry frying pan over a lowish heat. Keep your eye on them, though, as they can burn in the blink of an eye.

## Consiglio  **Fusilli, the spiral-shaped pasta, are equally good in this recipe and 250g/9oz of cooked spinach could be used instead of the broccoli and cauliflower.**

## Conchiglie con Salsa di Noci e Funghi Pasta Shells with Walnut and Mushroom Sauce serves 4

This wonderfully light and luscious recipe from the Parma region of Italy combines two of my all-time favourite flavours. Conchiglie are the familiar pasta shells which, because of their receptacle-like shape and the fact that they are ribbed, really mop up a sauce.

115g/4oz dried wild mushrooms, preferably porcini

350g/12oz conchiglie (pasta shells, see above)

sea salt and freshly ground black pepper

85g/3oz walnuts

handful of basil leaves

handful of young sage leaves

200ml/7fl oz single cream

1 large garlic clove

25g/1oz unsalted butter

50g/2oz freshly grated Parmesan cheese

1 Soak the dried mushrooms in warm water to cover for 10 minutes.

2 Meanwhile, cook the pasta in a large saucepan of boiling salted water until al dente, i.e. tender but still firm to the bite.

3 While the pasta cooks, finely chop the walnuts, tear the basil and chop the sage. Add the cream, season with salt and pepper, and mix together.

4 Crush the garlic. Drain the mushrooms and pat dry. Chop any that are too large. Melt the butter in a frying pan, add the garlic and fry it gently for 2–3 minutes. Stir in the mushrooms and cream sauce. Warm through gently.

5 Drain the cooked pasta and pour the mixture over it, stirring well. Serve sprinkled with Parmesan cheese.

### Variations

If you are lucky enough to get fresh walnuts, still in the shell, make a simple pasta with walnut sauce using this recipe but without the mushrooms. Replace the assertive basil and sage with a handful of chopped parsley to better set off the subtle flavour of the nuts, Store walnuts in the fridge or freezer to prevent them becoming rancid.

For a version of either dish with fewer fat calories, replace the cream with bread soaked in milk and whiz this with the nuts in the food processor until the nuts are finely chopped.

## Farfalle alla Crema di Gorgonzola Farfalle with Gorgonzola Cream    serves 4

In Italy, bow-tie-shaped farfalle is the next favourite pasta shape after spaghetti, as its captures so much sauce and cooks quickly. It is perfect for a dish in which you simply stir in sauce ingredients.

**350g/12oz dried farfalle**
sea salt and freshly ground black pepper
**175g/6oz Gorgonzola cheese (at room temperature), rind removed and cut into very small dice**
150ml/¼ pint double cream
**pinch of sugar**
2 tsp finely chopped fresh sage, plus fresh sage leaves, shredded, to garnish

1 Cook the pasta in a large pan of boiling salted water until just al dente, i.e. tender but still firm to the bite, 8–10 minutes.

2 Drain the cooked pasta well and return it to the pan in which it was cooked. Add the Gorgonzola, cream, sugar, plenty of black pepper and the chopped sage. Toss over a medium heat until the pasta is evenly coated. Taste and season with more salt if necessary.

3 Divide among 4 warmed bowls. Garnish each portion with sage and serve immediately

**Four cheeses** Instead of just the Gorgonzola, simply stir in 50g/2oz each Parmesan, Gruyère, Fontina and Gorgonzola (grate the first two and dice the others quite small) with the other additions.

**Ready-cooked prawns** Shell 350g/12oz large cooked prawns (200g/7oz if already peeled) and stir these into the pasta with 2 crushed garlic cloves, the grated zest of an unwaxed lemon and some flat-leaf parsley instead of the sage.

**Prosciutto and Gruyère cheese** Cut 8 slices of prosciutto (if you can, try to get them sliced a little thicker than usual) into strips and stir these into the pasta with 115g/4oz grated Gruyère cheese. The sage will still work well with this combination, but you may not need the sugar.

**Spinach and tomatoes** Rinse 500g/1lb 2oz of baby spinach leaves well and spin or pat dry. Deseed and chop 8 ripe tomatoes, preferably Italian. Sir these into the pasta, together with 2 crushed garlic cloves and some flat-leaf parsley instead of the sage.

# Fettuccine con Ceci Fettuccine with Chickpeas    serves 4

**This is a classic Neapolitan dish. Chickpeas are grown all over Italy but thrive in the south, where it is sunny. Although I think that dried pulses have more flavour and texture, canned are definitely quick and easy and make a good substitute. If you have the time and can cook fresh chickpeas, the flavour of this dish will be at its very best. However, bear in mind that the older the pulse, the longer it will take to cook and the flavour will not be as appetizing.**

sea salt and freshly ground black pepper

**350g/12oz fettuccine**

12 tasty flavoursome tomatoes or 200g/7oz vine-ripened cherry tomatoes

**4 tbsp olive oil**

2 garlic cloves, crushed

**generous handful chopped of flat-leaf parsley**

400g/14oz can of chickpeas, drained and rinsed

**2 tbsp fruity fine extra-virgin olive oil**

generous quantity of freshly grated Parmesan cheese, to serve

**generous handful of freshly torn basil, to serve**

1 Cook the pasta in a large pan of boiling salted water until just al dente, i.e. tender but still firm to the bite.

2 Meanwhile, put the tomatoes in a bowl, cover with boiling water for about 40 seconds then plunge them into cold water. Using a sharp knife, peel off the skins and chop the flesh. If using vine-ripened tomatoes, just halve.

3 Heat the olive oil in a medium-sized saucepan and gently cook the garlic. Add the tomatoes, parsley and chickpeas, salt and pepper. Cover and set aside.

4 Drain the pasta when ready and toss in the fruity fine extra-virgin olive oil and the chickpea mixture. Adjust the seasoning to taste.

5 Serve in warmed bowls with lashings of cheese and basil leaves.

## Variation

If you have the time to use dried chickpeas, soak 100g/3½oz dried chickpeas overnight in a bowl of cold water. The next day, drain and put in a large saucepan. Cover with fresh water, bring to the boil and boil for 10 minutes. Lower the heat and simmer for 20–30 minutes until tender. Drain well and use like the canned.

# Spaghetti alla Rancetto  Spaghetti with Tomatoes and Pancetta   serves 4

This traditional dish gets its name from a restaurant in **Spoleto** in Umbria. It uses a fresh and light sauce in which the tomatoes are cooked for a short time only. Always search out good flavoursome tomatoes, preferably from where the sun has been shining on them, as this will make the world of difference.

**350g/12oz ripe plum tomatoes**
150g/5oz pancetta, diced
**2 tbsp olive oil**
1 onion, finely chopped
**sea salt and freshly ground black pepper**
350g/12oz fresh or dried spaghetti
**handful of fresh marjoram sprigs, leaves stripped**
generous amount of freshly grated Pecorino cheese, to serve

1 Chop the ripe plum tomatoes into chunky dice.

2 Put the pancetta in a medium saucepan with the oil. Stir over a low heat until the fat runs. Add the onion and stir to mix. Cook gently for about 5 minutes, stirring.

3 Add the tomatoes with salt and pepper to taste. Stir well and cook for 7 minutes.

4 Meanwhile, cook the pasta a large pan of boiling salted water until just al dente, i.e. tender but still firm to the bite.

5 Remove the sauce from the heat and stir in the marjoram. Taste and adjust the seasoning if necessary.

6 Drain the pasta and tip into a warmed serving bowl. Pour the sauce over the pasta and toss well. Serve immediately in warmed bowls. Hand round the grated Pecorino separately.

## Variation
Very similar is Amatriciana, a classic tomato sauce named after the town of Amatrice in the Sabine Hills in Lazio. If you visit Rome, you will see it on so many restaurant menus, served with either bucatini or spaghetti. The addition of a fresh red chilli, deseeded and cut into thin strips, and replacing the marjoram with 2 or 3 tablespoons of dry white wine will give a good approximation of it.

## Consiglio  **Try to find pancetta; bacon can be substituted but the sauce will not taste the same. You can buy packets of ready-diced pancetta in most supermarkets. Alternatively you can buy it in a piece, sometimes cut from a roll (arrotolata), and dice it yourself.**

# Vermicelli allo Zafferano  Vermicelli with Saffron  serves 4

**This quick and easy dish makes a delicious midweek supper. The ingredients are likely to be sitting in the fridge, so it is also perfect for impromptu meals. Saffron strands are better than powder as they have much more flavour.**

**350g/12oz dried vermicelli**
sea salt and freshly ground black
pepper
**large pinch of saffron strands**
150g/5oz cooked ham, cut
into strips
**200ml/7fl oz double cream**
50g/2oz freshly grated Parmesan
cheese, plus extra to serve
**2 egg yolks**

1 Cook the vermicelli in a large saucepan of boiling salted water until just al dente, i.e. tender but still firm to the bite.

2 While the pasta is cooking, put the saffron strands in a saucepan, add 2 tablespoons of water and bring to the boil immediately. Remove the pan from the heat and leave it to sit for a while.

3 Add the ham to the pan containing the saffron, and stir in the cream and Parmesan with a little salt and pepper to taste. Heat gently, stirring all the time. When the cream starts to bubble, remove the sauce from the heat and add the egg yolks, beating well to mix. Taste and adjust the seasoning.

4 Add the drained vermicelli, mix well and serve in warmed bowls, with extra cheese if you wish.

## Variation
This dish is a really just a slightly smartened-up version of the classic Spaghetti alla Carbonara, named after the Roman charcoal workers who are said to have devised it. Without the glamorous touch of saffron and using the same way with ham or bacon, eggs and cheese, it became one of the earliest pasta dishes well known outside Italy, as it was a firm favourite among Allied soldiers in Italy in the Second World War, reminding them of their own homely breakfasts, so they took the recipe home with them.

# Spaghetti alla Carrettiera Spaghetti with Mushrooms, Pancetta and Tuna   serves 4

The term *carrettiera* means 'in the style of a cart driver', as this is the sort of robust meal they would have ordered at the trattoria at the end of a long journey. The Romans lay claim to the recipe, but so do the Neapolitans and Sicilians, hence there are many different versions of it.

25g / 1oz dried porcini mushrooms

175ml / 6fl oz warm water

2 tbsp olive oil

1 garlic clove

85g / 3oz pancetta or rindless streaky bacon, cut into 5mm / ¼in slices

225g / 8oz button mushrooms, chopped

sea salt and freshly ground black pepper

350g / 12oz dried spaghetti

200g / 7oz can of tuna (preferably in olive oil), drained

1 Put the porcini in a small bowl, pour over the warm water and leave to soak for 15 minutes.

2 Meanwhile, heat the oil in a large saucepan, add the garlic clove and cook gently for about 2 minutes, crushing it with a wooden spoon to release the flavour. Remove the garlic and discard. Add the pancetta or bacon to the oil remaining in the pan and cook for 3–4 minutes, stirring occasionally.

3 Drain the dried mushrooms, reserving the soaking liquid, and chop them finely.

4 Add both types of mushroom to the pan and cook, stirring, for 1–2 minutes, then add 6 tablespoons of the reserved mushroom soaking liquid, with salt and pepper to taste. Simmer for 5 minutes.

5 Meanwhile, cook the pasta in boiling salted water until al dente, i.e. just tender but still firm to the bite, adding the remaining mushroom soaking liquid to the pasta cooking water.

6 Flake the drained canned tuna into the mushroom sauce and fold it in gently. Taste and adjust the seasoning.

7 Drain the cooked pasta well and tip it into a warmed serving bowl. Pour the sauce over the top, toss well and serve immediately.

## Variation
You could replace the canned tuna with canned sardines – or even some grilled fresh ones if you felt like it,

## Maccheroni alla Bottarga di Favignana Macaroni with Dried Tuna Roe   serves 4

**Although this may seem an unusual recipe, with bottarga – salted and air-dried mullet or tuna roe – as the principal ingredient, it is very well known in Sardinia and also in Sicily and parts of southern Italy. It is simplicity itself to make and tastes very, very good. The raw garlic and pine nut *crema* with which the dish is dressed cuts the saltiness of the roe beautifully and can itself make a delicious dressing for plain pasta.**

350g/12oz maccheroni
sea salt and freshly ground black pepper
2 tbsp olive oil
1 garlic clove, sliced
10 cherry tomatoes, halved
½ glass of dry white wine
handful of flat-leaf parsley chopped
2 tbsp extra-virgin olive oil
85g/3oz bottarga di tonno (see Consiglio, right), diced very small

FOR THE CREMA
2 garlic cloves
25g/1oz pine nuts, preferably Italian

1 Cook the maccheroni in a large saucepan of boiling salted water for 10 minutes until just al dente, i.e. tender but still firm to the bite.

2 Meanwhile, make the crema: using a pestle and mortar, crush the garlic cloves and the pine nuts to a cream.

3 In a medium-sized saucepan, heat the olive oil and add the sliced garlic, the tomatoes and the wine. Stir-fry for 3 minutes, until the wine has been absorbed.

4 Drain the pasta when ready and toss with the parsley, extra-virgin olive oil and the bottarga. Add the tomato sauce and toss again.

5 Top with the crema and serve immediately.

### Variation
Although this dish suits the firm stubbiness of maccheroni incredibly well, you can also make a version with spaghetti and dress it with a garlic-infused oil instead of the crema.

Consiglio You can buy bottarga in Italian delicatessens. Small jars of ready-grated bottarga are convenient, but the best flavour comes from vacuum-packed slices of mullet bottarga, which are very easy to grate. Keep any leftover bottarga lightly wrapped in the fridge.

# per tutti i giorni

everyday

**4**

As I have said several times elsewhere in the book, like most Italians I don't regard it as a proper day unless I've had at least one plate of pasta. Everyday pasta is family fare, using the least expensive ingredients, such as seasonal vegetables and pulses. Flavouring ingredients like chillies and dried porcini also feature quite often, as they go a long way and deliver a lot of punch for pennies. Do not stint on buying the best and most flavourful oil, butter and cheese — as well, obviously, as good, tasty (m

# a con Piselli Pasta and Peas  serves 2

This simple *nonna* (grandmother)-style dish shows that the combination of peas and basil is as good as that of basil and tomato. Pappardelle are the wide pasta ribbons of the Veneto and Tuscany.

2 tbsp olive oil
I small onion, finely chopped
175g/6oz shelled fresh peas
600ml/1pint vegetable stock, preferably home made
150g/5oz pappardelle (see above)
sea salt and freshly ground black pepper
handful of torn fresh basil leaves
lashings of freshly grated Parmesan cheese

1 Heat the oil in a medium saucepan, add the onion and fry until soft.

2 Add the peas and stock, and cook for 10 minutes until the peas are soft.

3 Add the pasta, broken into pieces, with some salt and pepper to taste. Cook for about 12 minutes until the pasta is al dente, i.e. tender but still firm to the bite (it will absorb some of the stock).

4 Serve sprinkled with basil and Parmesan cheese.

Consiglio  To eat this at its best, use fresh new season's peas when they are sweet and tender.

# Pasta con Sugo di Verdure Pasta with Green Vegetable Sauce  serves 4

Although described as *sugo* in Italian, this is not a true sauce, because it does not have any liquid apart from the oil and melted butter. It is more a medley of vegetables to toss with freshly cooked pasta.

2 carrots
I courgette
85g/3oz French beans
I small leek
2 ripe Italian plum tomatoes
I handful of flat-leaf parsley
350g/12oz pasta of your choice
sea salt and freshly ground black pepper
25g/1oz butter
3 tbsp extra-virgin olive oil
½ tsp sugar
115g/4oz fresh peas

1 Dice the carrots and the courgette finely. Top and tail the French beans, then cut them into 2cm/$^3/_4$in lengths. Slice the leek thinly. Peel and dice the tomatoes. Chop the parsley and set aside.

2 Cook the pasta in a pan of salted boiling water until al dente, i.e. just tender but still firm to the bite.

3 Melt the butter with the oil in a medium-sized saucepan. When the mixture sizzles, add the prepared leek and carrots. Sprinkle the sugar over and fry, stirring frequently, for about 5 minutes.

4 Stir in the courgettes, French beans, peas and plenty of salt and pepper. Cover and cook over a low to medium heat, stirring occasionally, for 5–8 minutes, until the vegetables are tender.

5 Stir in the parsley and chopped plum tomatoes, and adjust the seasoning to taste. Serve at once, tossed with the freshly cooked pasta.

# Spaghetti alla Bellini Spaghetti with Mushrooms   serves 4

**This tasty dish is named after Pina Bellini, the celebrated proprietor of La Scaletta restaurant in Milan, famed for its handmade pasta.**

15g/½oz dried porcini mushrooms

175ml/6fl oz warm water

**3 tbsp olive oil**

2 garlic cloves, finely chopped

**handful of flat-leaf parsley, roughly chopped**

2 large pieces of drained sun-dried tomato in olive oil, sliced into thin strips

**125ml/4fl oz dry white wine**

225g/8oz chestnut mushrooms, thinly sliced

**450ml/¾ pint vegetable stock**

350g/12oz spaghetti

**sea salt and freshly ground black pepper**

handful of mixed chopped rocket and parsley, to garnish

1 Put the dried porcini mushrooms in a bowl, pour the warm water over and leave to soak for 15–20 minutes. Tip into a fine sieve set over a bowl and squeeze the porcini with your hands to release as much liquid as possible. Reserve the strained soaking liquid. Chop the porcini finely.

2 Heat the oil and cook the garlic, parsley, sun-dried tomato strips and porcini over a low heat, stirring frequently, for about 5 minutes.

3 Stir in the wine, simmer for a few minutes until reduced by half, then stir in the chestnut mushrooms. Pour in the stock and simmer, uncovered, for 15–20 minutes, until the liquid has reduced and the sauce is quite thick and rich.

4 While that simmers, cook the pasta in boiling salted water until al dente, i.e. tender but still firm to the bite.

5 Taste the mushroom sauce and adjust the seasoning if necessary. Drain the cooked pasta, reserving a little of the cooking liquid, and tip it into a warmed large bowl. Add the mushroom sauce and toss well, thinning the sauce if necessary with some of the pasta cooking water.

6 Serve immediately, sprinkled liberally with chopped rocket and parsley.

## Variation
To turn this everyday dish into a special-occasion treat, use mixed wild mushrooms, like fresh porcini (ceps), chanterelles and morels. You can also stir in some double cream at the last minute for an extra deluxe touch.

# Pizzocheri della Valtellina Pasta Layer with Cabbage, Beans and Potatoes    serves 6

**This substantial dish from Lombardy is well suited to fending off the Alpine chill. Buckwheat pasta is also popular in this part of the world as it is said to help stimulate the circulation.**

### FOR THE PASTA
300g/10½oz buckwheat flour
150g/5oz plain flour
3 eggs
7 tbsp milk
a little lukewarm water
pinch of salt

### FOR THE FILLING
200g/7oz potatoes
sea salt and freshly ground black pepper
225g/8oz mixture of equal parts French beans and Brussels sprouts or cabbage
70g/2½oz unsalted butter
1 garlic clove, crushed
freshly grated nutmeg
handful of fresh sage leaves
115g/4oz grated Fontina cheese
75g/3oz freshly grated Parmesan cheese

1 Make the pasta: sift both the flours into a mound on a work surface and make a hollow in the centre. Beat the eggs together and pour into the hollow with the milk, a little lukewarm water and the salt. Mix together to a smooth dough, then leave to stand for 10 minutes.

2 Roll out the dough to a paper-thin sheet. Roll it up from one long side and cut across into pieces about 1cm/½in wide; these will unroll into strips about 30cm/12in long.

3 To make the filling, peel the potatoes, cube them and cook in boiling salted water until tender. Chop the cabbage, if using. Steam the vegetables until tender.

4 Heat the butter in a saucepan, add the garlic and fry gently until softened. Add the nutmeg, sage and vegetables, and stir to coat the vegetables in the melted butter. Season well with salt and pepper..

5 Cook the pasta in a large saucepan of boiling salted water for 6 minutes until al dente, i.e. just tender but still firm to the bite. Drain well.

6 Put a layer of pasta in a large warmed serving dish followed by a layer of vegetables. Sprinkle with the cheeses. Repeat these layers and serve.

Consiglio   **As buckwheat pasta is hard to find, I've included a recipe for it. Buckwheat flour can be bought in most health food shops.**

# Brandelli con Melanzane e Zucchini Brandelli with Aubergine and Courgette Sauce serves 4

**Versions of this classic family dish are to be found all over southern Italy, where aubergines of all types are abundant.**

**200g / 7oz aubergine**
sea salt and freshly ground black pepper
**350g / 12oz brandelli (see Consiglio, below)**
**2 medium carrots**
**2 small courgettes**
I large onion
**4 tbsp olive oil**
2 garlic cloves, crushed
**I tbsp chopped fresh rosemary**
100ml / 3½fl oz red wine
**85g / 3oz freshly grated Pecorino cheese**

1 Peel the aubergine and chop the flesh into matchsticks. Put in a bowl and sprinkle with salt. Place a plate on top of the aubergine and weight down. Leave for 20 minutes.

2 Toward the end of this time, cook the pasta in a large saucepan of boiling salted water for about 12 minutes until al dente, i.e. just tender but still firm to the bite.

3 While the pasta cooks, cut the carrots and courgettes into matchsticks. Finely chop the onion. Rinse the aubergine matchsticks and pat dry.

4 Heat the olive oil in a saucepan, add the carrot, courgette and aubergine matchsticks and fry until golden. Add the onion and fry until coloured, then add the garlic and rosemary. Lower the heat and add the wine, with salt and pepper to taste. Simmer, covered, for 5 minutes.

5 Drain the cooked pasta and toss into the sauce. Serve sprinkled with the Pecorino cheese.

## Variation
Add a basic tomato sauce and some grated salted ricotta (see page 35) and you have something approximating to the famous pasta alla norma.

## Consiglio  **If the crinkled squares of brandelli are not available, you could use pappardelle or your favourite shape.**

# Conchiglie Grandi Farcite Stuffed Giant Pasta Shells   serves 2

These filled pasta shells are delicious on their own or they could be served with a white béchamel sauce. Toasting the pine nuts makes them far tastier. You could toast a large batch at a time and store them in a jar in the fridge to keep them fresh.

**12 giant pasta shells**

salt and freshly ground black pepper

**350g/12oz broccoli florets**

50g/2oz pine nuts

**225g/8oz Dolcelatte cheese**

1 garlic clove, crushed

**small handful of finely snipped fresh chives**

a little extra-virgin olive oil

**freshly grated Parmesan cheese, for sprinkling**

1 Cook the pasta shells in a large pan of boiling salted water for about 10 minutes until al dente, i.e. just tender but still firm to the bite.

2 While the pasta cooks, steam the broccoli florets for about 8 minutes until tender.

3 Toast the pine nuts on a sheet of foil under the grill, turning them frequently.

4 Put the steamed broccoli, Dolcelatte, pine nuts, garlic and chives in a bowl, with salt and pepper to taste, and mix together.

5 Drain the pasta and toss in a little olive oil to prevent the shells from sticking together. While still warm, stuff them with the filling.

6 Place the stuffed pasta shells in a greased shallow ovenproof serving dish, sprinkle over the Parmesan cheese and grill until bubbling. Serve immediately.

## Variation
These large pasta shells suit a whole range of different stuffings – try roasted peppers and tomatoes or ham and mushrooms with cheese.

# Conchiglie con Verdure Arrostite Conchiglie with Roasted Vegetables  serves 4

**Nothing could be simpler or more delicious than tossing freshly cooked pasta with roasted vegetables.**

**1 red pepper, deseeded and cut into 1cm/½in squares**
1 yellow pepper, deseeded and cut into 1cm/½in squares
**1 small aubergine, roughly diced**
2 courgettes, roughly diced
**5 tbsp extra-virgin olive oil**
handful of chopped fresh flat-leaf parsley
**1 tsp dried oregano**
sea salt and freshly ground black pepper
**250g/9oz cherry tomatoes, preferably on the vine, cut in half**
2 garlic cloves, roughly chopped
**350g/12oz conchiglie (see page 42)**
marjoram flowers or oregano flowers, to garnish (optional)

1 Preheat the oven to 190°C/375°F/Gas 5. Rinse the prepared peppers, aubergine and courgettes under running water. Drain, then lay the vegetables in a large roasting tin.

2 Pour 3 tablespoons of the olive oil over the vegetables and sprinkle with the fresh and dried herbs. Season to taste and stir well. Roast for about 30 minutes, stirring 2 or 3 times.

3 Stir the halved tomatoes and chopped garlic into the vegetable mixture and then roast for 20 minutes more, again stirring once or twice.

4 Meanwhile, cook the pasta in boiling salted water until al dente, i.e. tender but still firm to the bite.

5 Drain the cooked pasta and tip it into a warmed bowl. Add the roasted vegetables and the remaining oil, and toss well.

6 Serve the pasta and vegetables hot in warmed bowls, sprinkling each portion well with a few herb flowers if you have them.

## Variation
Try this dish with roast pumpkin, replacing the parsley and oregano with fresh sage leaves.

# Rigatoni Casalinga Country-style Rigatoni (with courgette, red onion and Gorgonzola)   **serves 4**

**This rustic dish suits all sorts of additions and variations — it's the sort of thing that you can heap leftover bacon, ham or chicken into and get great results every time. Be creative...**

**350g/12oz rigatoni (see page 41) or other pasta shape**
sea salt and freshly ground black pepper
**2 tender young courgettes**
1 red onion
**1 celery stalk**
8 stoned olives
**4 sun-dried tomatoes**
115g/4oz Gorgonzola cheese
**3 tbsp olive oil**
1 garlic clove, crushed
**glass of white wine**
large handful of fresh basil leaves
**freshly grated Parmesan cheese, to serve**

1 Cook the pasta in a large pan of boiling salted water for about 10 minutes until al dente, i.e. just tender but still firm to the bite.

2 While the pasta cooks, chop the courgettes into julienne strips. Finely chop the onion and celery. Roughly chop the olives and chop the tomatoes. Cut the gorgonzola cheese into cubes.

3 Steam the courgette strips for 2 minutes.

4 In a medium saucepan, heat the oil and fry the onion for about 5 minutes until soft. Add the celery, garlic and wine and simmer for 6 minutes.

5 Add the courgette strips, olives, tomatoes, cubed cheese, basil, and salt and pepper to taste, and stir together.

6 Drain the cooked pasta, add the sauce and toss together. Adjust the seasoning to taste and serve immediately with Parmesan cheese.

Consiglio  **The best sun-dried tomatoes are those without the seeds, because the seeds are bitter. Good sun-dried tomatoes should be slightly moist, sweet and tender.**

## Rigatoni con Aglio Arrostito, Peperoncino e Funghi
## Rigatoni with Roasted Garlic, Chilli and Mushrooms    serves 4

**Roasting garlic gives it an entirely different and much more complex flavour. Try a range of garlics and you will notice the subtle variations in their flavours.**

**2 whole garlic bulbs, plus 1 extra garlic clove, crushed**
2 tbsp olive oil, plus extra to drizzle
**1 red chilli**
300g / 10oz flat mushrooms
**350g / 12oz rigatoni (see page 41)**
sea salt and freshly ground black pepper
**150ml / ¼ pint double cream**
freshly grated Parmesan cheese to serve

1  Preheat the oven to 200°C/400°F/Gas 6. Slice the tops off the whole garlic bulbs and put in a roasting tin. Drizzle with a little oil and roast in the oven for 30 minutes, turning after 15 minutes. They will become golden and papery on the outside. Leave to cool slightly.

2  Finely chop the chilli, discarding the seeds. Roughly chop the mushrooms. Heat the olive oil in a frying pan, add the mushrooms and fry for 8 minutes. Add the chilli and the crushed garlic, and cook for a further 4 minutes.

3  Meanwhile, cook the pasta in boiling salted water until al dente, i.e. tender but still firm to the bite.

4  While the pasta is cooking, squeeze the roasted garlic cloves like toothpaste from a tube to extract the garlic pulp from each clove. Add the pulp to the mushroom mixture. Stir in the cream and add salt and pepper.

5  Drain the cooked pasta and pour over the sauce. Serve with the cheese

# cheroni con Broccoli in Tegame Macaroni with Broccoli and Cauliflower   serves 4

**This is a southern Italian dish, full of vibrant flavours.**

**175g/6oz cauliflower florets,
cut into small sprigs**

sea salt and freshly ground black
pepper

**175g/6oz broccoli florets, cut
into small sprigs**

350g/12oz short-cut macaroni

**3 tbsp olive oil**

1 onion, finely chopped

**3 tbsp pine nuts**

1 large pinch of saffron powder,
dissolved in 1 tbsp warm water

**1 tbsp raisins (optional)**

2 tbsp sun-dried tomato paste

**4 marinated anchovies, chopped,
plus extra to serve (optional)**

1 Cook the cauliflower sprigs in a large saucepan of boiling salted water for 3 minutes. Add the broccoli and boil both together for another 2 minutes. Remove the vegetables from the pan with a large slotted spoon and set aside.

2 Add the pasta to the vegetable cooking water an ... back to the boil. Cook the pasta until al dente, i.e. tender but still fi ... .e bite.

3 Meanwhile, heat the olive oil in a large skillet or s... pan, add the finely chopped onion and cook over a low-to-medium heat, ...rring frequent 2–3 minutes or until golden.

4 Add the pine nuts, the cooked broccoli and cauliflower, the saffron water, raisins if using, the sun-dried tomato paste and a couple of ladlefuls of the pasta cooking water until the vegetable mixture has the consistency of a sauce. Finally add plenty of pepper. Stir well.

5 Cook for 1–2 minute(s), then add the chopped anchovies.

6 Drain the cooked pasta and tip it into the vegetable mixture. Toss well, then taste and adjust the seasoning if necessary.

7 Serve the pasta immediately. You may like to add 1 or 2 whole anchovies on top of each serving.

Consiglio   **If you are using the raisins, try plumping them up in the saffron water (you may need to add another spoonful of water).**

# Spaghetti alla Siracusana Spaghetti with Anchovies and Olives serves 4

Named after Syracuse, the great Sicilian port, the strong flavours of this dish are typical of the island's cuisine.

3 tbsp olive oil

I large red pepper, deseeded and chopped

I small aubergi͏‌‍‍ ͏‌ely chopped

I oni͏‌ ͏‌y chopped

8 ripe ͏‌ ͏‌m tomatoes, skinn͏‌d, deseeded ͏‌ ͏‌ne͏‌y chopped

͏‌ garlic cloves, ͏‌ely chopped

125ml / 4fl oz dry red wine

handful of mixed basil, flat-leaf parsley and rosemary

sea salt and freshly ground black pepper

350g / 12oz dried spaghetti

50g / 2oz canned anchovies, roughly chopped, plus extra to garnish

12 pitted black olives

1–2 tbsp salt-packed capers, to taste

1 Heat the oil in a saucepan and add all the finely chopped vegetables and garlic. Cook gently, stirring frequently, for 10–15 minutes, until the vegetables are soft.

2 Pour in the wine and 125ml / 4fl oz water. Add the fresh herbs and pepper to taste, and bring to the boil. Lower the heat and simmer, stirring occasionally, for 10–15 minutes.

3 Meanwhile, cook the pasta in a pan of salted boiling water until al dente, i.e. just tender but still firm to the bite.

4 Add the chopped anchovies, olives and capers to the sauce. Heat through for a few minutes, taste and adjust the seasoning.

5 Drain the pasta and tip it into a warmed bowl. Pour the sauce over the pasta, toss well and serve immediately, garnished with the whole anchovies.

# Chitarra con Sardine e Pane Grattati Chitarra with Sardines and Breadcrumbs serves 4

Chitarra is an interesting pasta that looks like spaghetti from a distance but is square in section.

8 filleted sardines

4 tbsp olive oil

sea salt and freshly ground black pepper

400g / 14oz chitarra pasta (above)

2 garlic cloves, crushed

2 good handfuls of fresh herbs, such as parsley, basil, thyme, plus more parsley for garnish

115g / 4oz breadcrumbs, toasted

1 Preheat the grill to medium. Brush the sardines with 2 tablespoons of oil and season. Grill for 8 minutes on each side, then allow to cool.

2 Cook the pasta in a pan of salted boiling water until al dente, i.e. just tender but still firm to the bite.

3 Heat the remaining oil in a small pan, add the garlic and fry gently, being careful not to allow it to colour. Break up the sardines when cool enough to handle and add with the herbs. Toss well with the pasta and breadcrumbs.

4 Serve immediately in warmed bowls, topped with parsley to garnish.

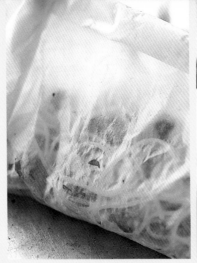

# Pasta al Cartoccio con Tonno, Pomodoro e Patate Pasta in parchment paper with tuna, tomatoes and potatoes serves 4

**Stunningly simple, this dish can be cooked ahead of time, is infinitely versatile and is a great family favourite with my sisters and their children. Italians have cooked in paper parcels for centuries, usually fish. It speeds up cooking and seals in all the flavour, nutrients and wonderful aromas.**

**250g/9oz tuna steak, chopped into 2cm/¾in cubes**
1 glass of white wine
**2 garlic cloves, finely chopped**
grated zest of 1 lemon
**2 sprigs of rosemary, broken into pieces**
sea salt and freshly ground black pepper
**8 new potatoes (preferably Italian), peeled and cut into small dice**
12 ripe plum tomatoes (preferably Italian), deseeded and roughly chopped
**handful of flat-leaf parsley, chopped, plus more to serve**
350g/12oz spaghetti
**2 tbsp olive oil**

1 Place the tuna in a bowl with the wine, garlic, lemon zest, rosemary and some seasoning. Leave to marinate for 30 minutes. Preheat the oven to 200°C/400°F/Gas 6.

2 Towards the end of marinating time, cook the potato dice in boiling salted water for 6 minutes until tender and drain. Combine with the tomatoes and parsley.

3 At the same time, half-cook the spaghetti (use just over half the time suggested on the packet). Drain.

4 In a large frying pan, heat the oil until hot, add the tuna with its marinade and fry very quickly for 6 minutes. Combine with the spaghetti, tomatoes and potato.

5 Mix the contents of the pan with the spaghetti, tomatoes and potato. Prepare 4 parcels with parchment paper, add one-quarter of the mixture to each and fold up loosely like an envelope. Fold in the edges and then fold over the top carefully to seal completely.

6 Place in the preheated oven for 7 minutes. Serve at once, slashing the bags at the table and sprinkling with more parsley.

## Courgette and courgette flowers

**In a little oil, gently cook 4 tender young courgettes, thinly sliced in rounds, with a finely chopped garlic clove, 2 tablespoons of dry white wine and some seasoning for 3 minutes until tender. Add a handful each of parsley and mint, followed by the 4 courgette flowers, cut into strips. Mix this with the spaghetti and make into parcels.**

## Tomatoes, olives, parsley and garlic

**Mix together 8 deseeded and chopped ripe plum tomatoes, 12 pitted and chopped fruity black olives, 2 finely chopped garlic cloves, a handful of chopped flat-leaf parsley and some seasoning. Mix this with the spaghetti and make into parcels.**

## Anchovies, capers and tomatoes

**Rinse 1 dessertspoon of capers (salt-packed for flavour) well and finely chop. Add 8 drained and chopped best-quality anchovies in oil, 8 deseeded and chopped ripe plum tomatoes, a handful of finely chopped flat-leaf parsley and a finely chopped garlic clove. Season with pepper only and mix well. Mix this with the spaghetti and make into parcels.**

## Broad beans, red onions, mint and Pecorino

**Sauté 2 sliced red onions in a little butter. Add 450g/1lb shelled broad beans with a handful of roughly chopped mint, a chopped garlic clove and seasoning. Cook, stirring frequently, until the beans are just tender. Allow to cool, then add 100g/3½oz freshly grated Pecorino (preferably Romano) to make a sauce. Mix this with the spaghetti and make into parcels.**

# Farfalle con Pollo e Pomodorini Farfalle with Chicken and Cherry Tomatoes   serves 4

**I have done this using leftover roast turkey (cooking only enough to warm through) to great acclaim.**

**350g/12oz skinless chicken breast fillets, cut into bite-sized pieces**

4 tbsp Italian dry vermouth

**2 tsp chopped fresh rosemary, plus 4 fresh rosemary sprigs to garnish**

sea salt and freshly ground black pepper

**I tbsp olive oil**

I onion, finely chopped

**85g/3oz piece of Italian salami, diced**

275g/10oz dried farfalle (see page 45)

**I tbsp balsamic vinegar**

400g/14oz can of Italian cherry tomatoes

**good pinch of crushed dried red chillies**

1 Put the pieces of chicken in a large bowl, pour over the dry vermouth and sprinkle with half the chopped rosemary and salt and pepper to taste. Stir well and set aside.

2 Heat the oil in a large saucepan, add the onion and salami, and fry over a medium heat for about 5 minutes, stirring frequently.

3 Meanwhile, cook the pasta in a pan of salted boiling water until al dente, i.e. just tender but still firm to the bite.

4 Add the chicken and vermouth to the onion and salami, increase the heat to high and fry for 3 minutes, or until the chicken is white on all sides. Sprinkle the vinegar over the chicken. Add the cherry tomatoes and dried chillies, stir well and simmer for a few minutes more. Taste the sauce and adjust the seasoning if necessary.

5 Drain the pasta and tip it into the sauce. Add the remaining chopped rosemary and toss to mix the pasta and sauce together. Serve immediately, in warmed bowls garnished with rosemary sprigs.

## Variation
Instead of chicken, try using well-trimmed chicken livers.

# Penne alla Rusticana Penne with Chicken, Broccoli and Cheese   serves 4

**Quick to prepare and easy to cook, this colourful dish is full of flavour.**

**115g/4oz broccoli florets, divided into tiny sprigs**

sea salt and freshly ground black pepper

**50g/2oz unsalted butter**

2 skinless chicken breast fillets, cut into thin strips

**2 garlic cloves, crushed**

400g/14oz dried penne (see page 39)

**125ml/4fl oz dry white wine**

200ml/7fl oz double cream

**85g/3oz Gorgonzola cheese, rind removed and cut into small dice**

freshly grated Parmesan cheese, to serve

1 Plunge the broccoli into a saucepan of boiling salted water. Bring back to the boil and boil for 2 minutes, then drain in a colander and refresh in cold water. Shake well to remove surplus water and set aside to drain completely.

2 Melt the butter in a large saucepan, add the chicken and garlic with salt and pepper to taste, and stir well. Fry over a medium heat for 3 minutes or until the chicken becomes white.

3 Meanwhile, cook the pasta in a pan of salted boiling water until al dente, i.e. just tender but still firm to the bite.

4 Pour the wine and cream over the chicken mixture in the pan and stir to mix, then simmer, stirring occasionally, for about 5 minutes until the sauce has reduced and thickened. Add the broccoli, increase the heat and toss to heat it through, then mix it with the chicken. Taste and adjust the seasoning if necessary.

5 Drain the pasta and tip it into the sauce. Add the Gorgonzola and toss well. Serve with grated Parmesan.

## Variation
For an even more substantial dish, add some sliced pancetta and chopped fresh sage with the chicken.

# Eliche con Salsiccia e Radicchio Eliche with Sausage and Radicchio serves 4

**This robust and hearty flavour combination is from Treviso in the north, where lots of radicchio is grown. Eliche are the pasta spirals that look more like screw-threads or propellers than fusilli.**

**2 tbsp olive oil**
I onion, finely chopped
**200g / 7oz Italian pure pork sausage**
175ml / 6fl oz passata
**6 tbsp dry white wine**
sea salt and freshly ground black pepper
**350g / 12oz dried eliche (see above)**
50g / 2oz radicchio leaves

1 Heat the olive oil in a large deep saucepan, add the finely chopped onion and cook over a low heat, stirring frequently, for about 5 minutes until softened.

2 Cut the sausage into bite-sized chunks and add to the pan. Stir to mix with the oil and onion and continue to fry the mixture, increasing the heat if necessary, until the sausage is well browned all over.

3 Stir in the passata, then sprinkle in the wine with salt and pepper to taste. Simmer over a low heat, stirring occasionally, for 10–12 minutes.

4 Meanwhile, cook the pasta in a pan of salted boiling water until al dente, i.e. just tender but still firm to the bite.

5 Just before draining the pasta, add a ladleful or two of the cooking water to the sausage sauce and stir well. Taste the sauce and adjust the seasoning if necessary. Slice the radicchio leaves thinly.

6 Drain the cooked pasta and tip it into the pan of sausage sauce. Add the shredded radicchio and toss well to combine everything together. Serve immediately.

## Variation
If you can't find Italian sausages, use Cumberland, Toulouse or even some of the tasty rare-breed pig sausages now becoming more common in our supermarkets.

# Bucatini alla Posillipo Bucatini with Sausage and Pancetta serves 4

**Named after a restaurant in Palermo, Sicily, this is a rich and satisfying dish. It hardly needs grated Parmesan cheese as an accompaniment, but you can hand some round in a separate bowl if you wish.**

115g/4oz pork sausage meat
400g/14oz can of Italian plum tomatoes
1 tbsp olive oil
1 garlic clove, crushed
115g/4oz pancetta or rindless streaky bacon, roughly chopped
handful of chopped fresh flat-leaf parsley
sea salt and freshly ground black pepper
400g/14oz dried bucatini (see page 40)
4–5 tbsp double cream
2 egg yolks

1 Remove any skin from the sausage meat and break the meat up roughly with a knife. Purée the tomatoes in a food processor or blender.

2 Heat the oil in a medium saucepan, add the garlic and fry over a low heat for 1–2 minutes. Remove the garlic with a slotted spoon and discard it.

3 Add the sausagemeat and pancetta or bacon, and cook over a medium heat for 3–4 minutes. Stir constantly with a wooden spoon to break up the sausagemeat – it will become brown and look crumbly.

4 Add the puréed tomatoes to the pan with half the parsley and salt and pepper to taste. Stir well and bring to the boil, scraping up any sediment that has stuck to the bottom of the pan. Lower the heat, cover and simmer for 20 minutes, stirring from time to time. Taste and adjust the seasoning, if necessary.

5 Meanwhile, cook the pasta in boiling salted water until al dente, i.e. tender but still firm to the bite.

6 Put the cream and egg yolks in a warmed large bowl and mix with a fork, seasoning with salt and pepper. As soon as the pasta is cooked, drain it well and add it to the bowl of cream mixture. Toss until the pasta is coated, then pour the sausagemeat sauce over the pasta and toss again.

7 Serve immediately in warmed bowls, sprinkled with the remaining parsley.

## Consiglio
**To save time puréeing the tomatoes, use passata. For authenticity, buy *salsiccia a metro*, a pure pork sausage sold by the metre at Italian delicatessens. Bucatini is a long, hollow pasta that looks like hard drinking straws; spaghetti works equally well.**

# Tagliatelle verdi al Sugo di Piselli Green tagliatelle with Fresh Pea Sauce   serves 4

**Here tagliatelle are used, but other pasta shapes, say farfalle, will work just as well. The use of pasta verde (spinach pasta) is very much a northern Italian thing.**

**1 tbsp olive oil**
**5–6 rindless rashers of streaky bacon, cut into strips**
**400g/14oz can of chopped Italian plum tomatoes**
sea salt and freshly ground black pepper
**350g/12oz dried tagliatelle verde**
225g/8oz peas, preferably freshly shelled or frozen at a pinch
**50g/2oz mascarpone cheese**
few basil leaves, freshly torn, plus more whole leaves, to garnish
**freshly grated Parmesan cheese**

1 Heat the oil in a medium saucepan and add the bacon. Cook over a low heat, stirring frequently, for 5–7 minutes.

2 Add the tomatoes and 4 tablespoons of water with salt and pepper to taste. Bring to the boil, lower the heat, cover and simmer gently for about 15 minutes, stirring from time to time.

3 Meanwhile, cook the pasta in boiling salted water until al dente, i.e. tender but still firm to the bite.

4 Add the peas to the tomato sauce, stir well to mix and bring to the boil. Cover the pan and cook for 5–8 minutes, until the peas are cooked and the sauce is quite thick. Taste and adjust the seasoning if necessary.

5 Turn off the heat under the pan and add the mascarpone and basil. Mix well. Cover the pan and leave to stand for 1–2 minutes.

6 Drain the pasta and tip it into a warmed bowl. Pour the sauce over the pasta and toss well.

7 Serve immediately, garnished with basil leaves, and hand round some grated Parmesan separately.

Consiglio **This sauce is more usually served with plain white pasta. The red, green and white make it _tricolore_, the colours of the Italian flag.**

# 5 leggero e sano
light & healthy

Pasta itself is basically high in complex carbohydrates and low in fat, and it is only the sauces that might introduce high levels of fats. What is more, the primary fat in pasta sauces tends to be healthy olive oil. You can also, as in this chapter, make a point of including foods that contain plant chemicals that are positively good for you, like broccoli and — of course — tomatoes, which both help protect against cancer and heart disease.

# Spaghetti con Pomodorini Spaghetti with Tiny Tomatoes  serves 2

The tomato is at the heart of many pasta sauces and it is perhaps no coincidence as it is now known that the lycopenes in which it is so rich are potent agents against heart disease and many types of cancer. Moreover, these powers seem to get even stronger when the tomato is cooked. I always try to buy Italian tomatoes, as they are full of sunshine and this gives them much more flavour.

**450g/1lb cherry tomatoes**
3 large garlic cloves, cut into slivers
**sea salt and freshly ground black pepper**
200g/7oz spaghetti
**1 small hot chilli pepper, deseeded and chopped (optional)**
1 tbsp olive oil for the chilli, if necessary
**handful of fresh basil, torn**
2 tbsp extra-virgin olive oil
**freshly grated Parmesan cheese, to serve**

1 Preheat the oven to 150°C/300°F/Gas 2. Cut the tomatoes in half and put on a baking sheet. Place a sliver of garlic on top of each, followed by a sprinkling of salt. Bake for 1¼ hours until dry but still squashy.

2 Cook the pasta in boiling salted water for about 10 minutes until al dente, i.e. just tender but still firm to the bite. If using the chilli, fry it in olive oil just long enough to colour it, then remove it from the heat.

3 Drain the pasta and stir in the tomatoes, chilli if using, basil and extra-virgin olive oil, with salt and pepper to taste.

4 Serve sprinkled with the cheese.

Consiglio  **The last person to be served is the luckiest, as they get the most sauce.**

# Penne con Pomodori Gratinati Penne with Gratinéed Tomatoes   serves 4

The region of **Campania** has been blessed with all of the proper elements for growing fruit and vegetables of unique quality – rich volcanic soil, a profusion of bright sunlight and a gentle climate – and the diet of the region relies heavily on them. The goodness of **Campania's San Marzano** tomato, a thick-fleshed cooking tomato, is hailed around the world. When I am teaching, I also refer to this tomato as the one 'with shoulders', meaning that it has an attitude, because it has such a unique flavour.

**3 tbsp olive oil**
125g/4½oz salt-packed capers
**2 medium garlic cloves**
16 large plum tomatoes, cored, cut in half lengthwise and deseeded
**25g/1oz dry breadcrumbs**
350g/12oz penne (see page 39)
**sea salt and freshly ground black pepper**
2 tbsp fine fruity extra-virgin olive oil
**handful of basil, freshly torn**

1 Preheat the oven to 150°C/300°F/Gas 2 and grease two 33 x 23cm/13 x 9in baking sheets with a little of the olive oil.

2 Soak the capers in 3 changes of cold water to remove the salt. Drain and pat them dry with paper towels.

3 Combine the capers and garlic on a cutting board and finely chop them together.

4 Arrange the tomatoes, cut side up, on the baking sheets. Sprinkle the mixture over the tomatoes, drizzle with the remaining olive oil and then sprinkle with the breadcrumbs. Roast for 45 minutes or until the tomatoes are very soft but still holding their shape.

5 Cook the pasta in boiling salted water for about 10 minutes until al dente, i.e. just tender but still firm to the bite. Drain and transfer to a large warm serving bowl. Spoon over the tomatoes and the extra-virgin olive oil, then sprinkle with some pepper and the basil.

6 Serve immediately in warmed bowls. Pass a bowl of freshly grated Parmesan cheese round to sprinkle on top.

## Variation
Instead of the capers, you can add piquancy with a small tin of anchovy fillets, drained. Either way, a chopped deseeded chilli also adds a bit of zing.

## Penne con Salsa di Melanzane Penne with Aubergine Sauce

**serves 4**

I medium aubergine

sea salt and freshly ground black pepper

**3 tbsp olive oil**

4 tbsp red wine

**I small onion, finely chopped**

400g/14oz canned chopped tomatoes

**I garlic clove, crushed**

350g/12oz penne (see page 39)

**2 tbsp double cream**

I tbsp finely chopped fresh oregano

**freshly grated Parmesan cheese, to serve (optional)**

1 Cut the aubergine into medium-sized cubes. Sprinkle with salt, place in a bowl, cover and weigh down. Leave for 15 minutes. This helps break down the cells so that the aubergine will absorb less oil in cooking and also helps draw out any of the bitterness that you might find in older specimens.

2 Rinse the aubergine and dry. Heat the oil in a frying pan, add the aubergine and fry for 5 minutes until golden. Add the wine and simmer for 15 minutes.

3 Add the onion and tomatoes to the aubergine, bring to the boil and simmer for 10 minutes. Add the garlic at this point.

4 While the sauce is simmering, cook the pasta in boiling salted water until al dente, i.e. just tender but still firm to the bite.

5 Just before serving, stir the cream and oregano into the sauce. Drain the pasta and toss with the sauce. Serve at once, with Parmesan cheese if you want.

## Garganelli con Verdure di Stagione Garganelli with Spring Vegetables

**serves 4**

**3 tbsp olive oil**

2 medium carrots, diced

**I celery stalk, diced**

I garlic clove, peeled and crushed

**I small red onion, chopped**

2 small courgettes, diced

**115g/4oz freshly shelled peas**

2 ripe tomatoes, diced

**I tsp fresh thyme leaves**

handful of fresh basil leaves, torn

**handful of freshly chopped flat-leaf parsley**

sea salt and freshly ground black pepper

**350g/12oz garganelli (ridged, pointed tubes, see page 138)**

2 tbsp double cream

**grated Parmesan cheese, to serve**

1 Heat the oil in a deep sauté pan and sauté the carrots, celery, garlic, onion, courgettes and peas over a low heat, stirring frequently, for 10 minutes or until tender. Add the tomatoes, cover and cook over a low heat for about 6 minutes, then add the herbs and salt and pepper to taste.

2 Cook the garganelli in boiling salted water until al dente, i.e. just tender but still firm to the bite, 7–10 minutes.

3 Toss the drained pasta in the vegetable sauce, adding cream and cheese to taste.

4 Serve immediately.

## Conchiglie con Salsa di Finocchio e Pomodoro
# Conchiglie with Fennel and Tomato Sauce   serves 4

**Fennel is said to cleanse the system, especially the liver.**

**2 medium fennel bulbs**
3 tbsp olive oil
**I garlic clove**
400g/14oz can chopped tomatoes
**grated zest of I unwaxed lemon**
handful of mint, chopped
**350g/12oz conchiglie (pasta shells, see page 42)**
sea salt and freshly ground black pepper
**freshly grated Parmesan cheese, to serve**

1 Preheat the oven to 200°C/400°F/Gas 6.

2 Remove the fennel's tough outer leaves and tough core, and wash well. Cut into lengths and steam or cook in boiling water for 7–8 minutes until tender. Transfer to a roasting tin and drizzle over a tablespoon of olive oil. Roast in the oven for 15 minutes until golden.

3 Meanwhile, crush the garlic. Heat the remaining olive oil in a saucepan, add the garlic and fry gently until softened. Add the tomatoes, lemon zest and mint, and cook gently for 25 minutes.

4 Towards the end of this time, cook the pasta in boiling salted water until al dente, i.e. just tender but still firm to the bite.

5 Chop the roast fennel into small pieces and add to the sauce. Season well with salt and pepper and heat gently.

6 Drain the cooked pasta and toss with the sauce. Serve hot, with plenty of grated Parmesan cheese.

# Spaghetti con Castagne e Salvia Spaghetti with Chestnuts and Sage   serves 4

500g/1lb 2oz chestnuts, preferably fresh, with a slit on each one

2 tbsp olive oil

2 garlic cloves, roughly chopped

handful of flat-leaf parsley, chopped

generous handful of roughly chopped sage

250g/9oz tinned chopped tomatoes

sea salt and freshly ground black pepper

350g/12oz spaghetti

freshly grated Parmesan cheese, to serve (optional)

1 Preheat the oven to 200°C/400°F/Gas 6. Place the slashed chestnuts in a medium saucepan with enough water to cover. Bring to the boil and boil for 10 minutes. Drain, place on a roasting sheet and roast in the oven for 35 minutes. Allow to cool, then peel and chop.

2 Heat the olive oil in a medium saucepan. Add the garlic, parsley, sage and tomatoes, and simmer very gently, covered, for 15 minutes. Add the roasted chestnuts and some seasoning, and simmer for 10 more minutes.

3 Meanwhile, cook the pasta in a large saucepan of boiling salted water until al dente, i.e. just tender but still firm to the bite.

4 Adjust the seasoning of the sauce, then drain the pasta and stir in the sauce, mixing well. Serve immediately, with Parmesan cheese if you wish.

# Pasta Vesuvio Pasta Vesuvius   serves 2

This is obviously named for its hot and fiery flavour. If you don't like hot food, it is still quite delicious without the chilli. Use single cream for a lighter dish and mascarpone for authenticity.

4 tomatoes

200g/7oz fettuccine

sea salt and freshly ground black pepper

25g/1oz stoned black or green olives

25g/1oz capers, well rinsed

1 tbsp olive oil

1 garlic clove, crushed

½ dried chilli, deseeded and chopped

handful of flat-leaf parsley, finely chopped, plus more whole sprigs, to garnish

handful of fresh mint, finely chopped, plus more whole sprigs, to garnish

2 tbsp mascarpone cheese or single cream

2 tsp freshly grated Parmesan cheese

1 Put the tomatoes in a bowl, cover with boiling water for about 40 seconds then plunge into cold water. Using a sharp knife, peel off the skins and chop the flesh, discarding the seeds.

2 Cook the pasta in a large saucepan of boiling salted water for 10 minutes until just al dente, i.e. just tender but still firm to the bite.

3 Meanwhile, finely chop the olives and capers. Heat the oil in a saucepan and fry the garlic until softened. Add the olives, capers, tomatoes, chilli, parsley and mint, and fry gently for about 5 minutes. Add the mascarpone cheese with salt and pepper to taste.

4 Drain the pasta, add to the pan and toss together with Parmesan cheese. Garnish with sprigs of fresh mint and parsley to serve.

Consiglio For a special occasion, when you are not so concerned with fat and calories, you can add a little double cream to the sauce at the end of Step 3.

# Trenette alla Genovese Trenette with Pesto, French Beans and Potatoes   serves 2

**In Liguria it is traditional to serve pesto with trenette, French beans and diced potatoes. The ingredients for making pesto are quite expensive, so the French beans and potatoes are added to help make the pesto go further. The people of Genoa are notoriously frugal.**

**2 potatoes (about 250g / 9oz)**
100g / 3½oz French beans
**sea salt and freshly ground black pepper**
350g / 12oz dried trenette (see below)

**FOR THE PESTO**
**very generous handful of fresh basil leaves**
2 garlic cloves, thinly sliced
1½ tbsp pine nuts
3 tbsp freshly grated Parmesan cheese, plus extra to serve
**2 tbsp freshly grated Pecorino cheese**
4 tbsp extra-virgin olive oil
**pinch of salt**

1 First make the pesto: put the basil leaves, garlic, pine nuts and cheeses in a blender or food processor and process for about 5 seconds. Add half of the oil and a pinch of salt and process for 5 seconds more. Stop the machine, remove the lid and scrape down the side of the bowl. Add the remaining oil and process for 5–10 seconds.

2 Cut the potatoes in half lengthwise, then cut each half across into 5mm / ¼in thick slices. Cut the beans into 2cm / ¾in pieces. Plunge the potatoes and beans into a large saucepan of salted boiling water and boil, uncovered, for 5 minutes.

3 Add the pasta, bring the water back to the boil, stir well, then cook for 5–7 minutes or until the pasta is al dente, i.e. just tender but still firm to the bite.

4 Meanwhile, put the pesto in a large bowl and add 3–4 tablespoons of the water used for cooking the pasta. Mix well.

5 Drain the pasta and vegetables, add to the pesto and toss well. Serve immediately on warmed plates with extra grated Parmesan and Pecorino handed round separately.

Consiglio   **Don't worry if the potatoes break up during cooking, as this will add to the creaminess of the finished dish.**

**The pesto can be made up to 2–3 days in advance and kept in a bowl in the fridge until needed. Pour a thin layer of olive oil over the top and cover the bowl lightly with cling film before refrigerating.**

**Trenette is the traditional Ligurian pasta that is served with pesto, but if you find it difficult to obtain you can use bavette or linguine instead. The two-coloured *paglia e fieno* (straw and hay) noodles would be another good choice.**

# Pasta con Calabrese Pasta with Broccoli  serves 2

**Some of the best broccoli is grown in the south of Italy, hence its other name, calabrese – from Calabria. Here I've combined it with pasta and homemade toasted breadcrumbs. To make the breadcrumbs, spread day-old breadcrumbs on a baking sheet and bake in an oven preheated to 190°C/375°F/Gas 5, stirring frequently, for about 10 minutes until golden.**

**200g/7oz ditali (short macaroni)**
sea salt and freshly ground black pepper
**375g/13oz broccoli**
**3–4 bay leaves**
**50g/2oz stoned green olives**
**2 tbsp olive oil**
**1 garlic clove, finely chopped**
**50g/2oz ground almonds**
**3 tbsp freshly toasted breadcrumbs (see above)**
extra-virgin olive oil, to serve
**freshly grated Parmesan cheese, to serve**

1 Cook the pasta in a large saucepan of boiling salted water for about 10 minutes until al dente, i.e. just tender but still firm to the bite.

2 While the pasta is cooking, cut the broccoli into florets and steam with the bay leaves for about 6 minutes until tender.

3 While the pasta and broccoli are cooking, finely chop the olives. Heat the oil and garlic in a frying pan, add the olives and ground almonds, and heat very gently, adding a tablespoon of water.

4 Drain the cooked pasta, toss in the broccoli, olive mixture and breadcrumbs, and mix well together. Drizzle over some extra-virgin olive oil and serve with Parmesan cheese.

## Consiglio  Broccoli is probably the healthiest of vegetables.
**It is high in fibre, packed full of the antioxidant vitamins beta-carotene and vitamin C, which help fight heart disease and cancer, and 'phytochemicals' called glucosinolates which also help protect against a range of cancers by stimulating the body's natural defences.**

**Tearing a fresh bay leaf helps release its aroma and flavour.**

# Orecchiette con Rucola Orecchiette with Rocket  serves 4

**This hearty dish is from Puglia in the south-east of Italy.**

**3 tbsp olive oil**
I small onion, finely chopped
**350g/12oz chopped plum**
**tomatoes or passata**
½ tsp dried oregano
**pinch of chilli flakes**
about 2 tbsp white wine (optional)
**sea salt and freshly ground black**
**pepper**
350g/12oz dried orecchiette
(page 102)
**2 garlic cloves, finely chopped**
150g/5oz rocket leaves, stalks
removed and leaves shredded
**45g/1½oz ricotta cheese**
freshly grated Pecorino cheese,
to serve

1 Heat I tablespoon of the olive oil in a medium saucepan, add half the finely chopped onion and cook gently, stirring frequently, for about 5 minutes until softened. Add the tomatoes, oregano and chilli flakes to the onion, pour over the wine if using and add a little salt and pepper to taste. Cover the pan and simmer for about 15 minutes, stirring occasionally.

2 Meanwhile, cook the pasta in a large saucepan of boiling salted water for about 15 minutes until al dente, i.e. just tender but still firm to the bite.

3 Heat the remaining oil in a large saucepan, add the rest of the onion and the garlic, and fry for 2–3 minutes, stirring occasionally. Add the rocket, toss over the heat for about 2 minutes until wilted, then stir in the tomato sauce and the ricotta. Mix well.

4 Drain the pasta, add to the pan of sauce and toss to mix. Taste and adjust the seasoning if necessary. Serve immediately in warmed bowls with grated Pecorino handed round separately.

## Seven deadly sins (wild herbs) Mix together
a small handful each of parsley, basil, thyme, rosemary,
sage, oregano and marjoram, and chop them all finely.
Stir all the chopped herbs into the pasta instead of the
rocket, omitting the dried oregano.

## Sun-dried tomatoes and radicchio Cut about
10 drained sun-dried tomatoes in oil into strips and shred
a large head of radicchio, preferably Treviso. Stir both of
these into the pasta instead of the rocket.

## Baby spinach and blue cheese Cut 200g/7oz
Gorgonzola picante into small cubes. Stir these and
about 350g/12oz of young spinach leaves into the
pasta instead of the rocket and omit the ricotta.

## Aubergines Cut a large aubergine into smallish cubes
and salt and rinse these as described on page 87. Stir
them into the pasta instead of the rocket.

# Linguine con Vongole e Cime di Rape Linguine with Clams and Turnip Tops   serves 4

**Humble turnip greens have long been popular in Italy and they are beginning to be rediscovered here. If you can't find them, do press your greengrocer or supermarket enquiry desk to get them in. It's what I have done and now they sell them to all comers. Linguine are the noodles that are oval in section, looking a bit like a flattened spaghetti.**

**625g / 1½lb Venus clams or**
**vongole verace**
a little plain flour
**2 tbsp olive oil**
2 leeks, thinly sliced
**2 fresh bay leaves**
1 garlic clove, crushed
**200ml / 7fl oz dry white wine**
sea salt and freshly ground
black pepper
**350g / 12oz linguine (see above)**
350g / 12oz turnip tops (cime di
rape), finely chopped
**3 tbsp roughly chopped**
**flat-leaf parsley**

1 Keep the clams submerged in water with a little added plain flour (this helps plump them up and purge them of any dirt). Discard any open ones that don't close when tapped.

2 Heat the oil in a large saucepan, add the leeks and bay leaves, and fry over a high heat until the leeks have some colour. Add the garlic and wine, salt and pepper to taste and the drained clams. Cover and cook over a medium-high heat for about 6 minutes, until all the clams open (discard any that don't).

3 At the same time, cook the linguine in a large saucepan of boiling salted water until al dente. Drain.

4 Remove the lid from the clam pan and throw in the rape, chard or spinach, and stir. Add the drained linguine and the parsley. Mix well, adjust the seasoning and serve immediately.

## Variation
If you can't find turnip tops, use Swiss chard or spinach instead.

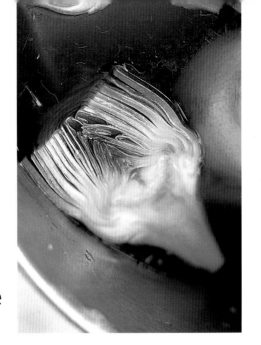

# Penne ai Gamberi e Carciofi Penne with Prawns and Artichokes  serves 4

This is a good dish to make in late spring or early summer, when green-purple baby artichokes appear in shops and market stalls. I have a great fondness for artichokes; they taste so wonderful and are really good for your liver as a cleanser. All Italians are obsessed with their livers, claiming it to be the 'happy organ'.

juice of 1 lemon

4 baby globe artichokes, preferably with good long stalks

3 tbsp olive oil

2 garlic cloves, crushed

handful of chopped fresh mint

handful of chopped fresh flat-leaf parsley

sea salt and freshly ground black pepper

350g/12oz dried penne (see page 39)

16 peeled cooked king or tiger prawns, preferably still with their tail shells attached

2 tbsp fruity fine extra-virgin olive oil

1 Have ready a pan of cold water to which you have added the lemon juice. To prepare the artichokes, cut off most of the artichoke stalks, if any, and cut across the tops of the leaves. Peel off and discard any tough or discoloured outer leaves. Cut the artichokes lengthwise into quarters and remove any hairy chokes from their centres. Put the pieces of artichoke in the pan of acidulated water to help prevent browning. Bring to the boil and simmer gently for about 10 minutes.

2 Drain the pieces of artichoke and pat them dry. Heat the olive oil in a nonstick frying pan and add the artichokes, the crushed garlic and half the mint and parsley to the pan. Season with plenty of salt and pepper, and cook over a low heat, stirring frequently, for about 3–4 minutes or until the artichokes are just tender.

3 Meanwhile, cook the pasta in a large saucepan of boiling salted water until al dente, i.e. just tender but still firm to the bite.

4 Add the prawns to the artichokes, stir well to mix, then heat through gently for 2 minutes.

5 Drain the cooked pasta and tip into a warmed bowl. Dress with the extra-virgin olive oil, spoon the artichoke mixture over the pasta and toss to combine.

6 Serve immediately, sprinkled with the remaining mint and parsley.

# Orecchiette con Acciughe e Broccoli Orecchiette with Anchovies and Broccoli   serves 4

**With its robust flavours, this pasta is typical of Puglia, southern Italy, and, in fact, Sicily. Anchovies, pine nuts, garlic and Pecorino cheese are all very popular ingredients there. Serve with crusty bread to mop up the juices.**

**350g/12oz broccoli florets**
sea salt and freshly ground black pepper
**25g/1oz pine nuts**
350g/12oz dried orecchiette (see below)
**2 tbsp olive oil**
1 small red onion, thinly sliced
**50g/2oz jar of anchovies in olive oil, drained**
1 garlic clove crushed
**25g/1oz freshly grated Pecorino cheese**

1 Break the broccoli florets into small sprigs and cut off the stalks. If the stalks are large, chop or slice them. Cook the broccoli florets and stalks in a saucepan of boiling salted water for 2 minutes, then drain and refresh in cold water. Leave to drain on kitchen paper.

2 Put the pine nuts in a dry nonstick frying pan and toss over a low to medium heat for 1–2 minutes until the nuts are lightly toasted. Remove and set aside.

3 Cook the pasta in a large saucepan of boiling salted water until al dente, i.e. just tender but still firm to the bite.

4 Meanwhile, heat the oil in a frying pan, add the onion and fry gently, stirring frequently, for about 5 minutes until softened. Add the anchovies, followed by the garlic, and cook over a medium heat until the anchovies break down to a paste. Add the broccoli and plenty of pepper and toss over the heat for a minute or two until the broccoli is hot. Taste and adjust the seasoning.

5 Drain the cooked pasta and tip into a warm bowl. Add the broccoli mixture and grated Pecorino, and toss well to combine. Sprinkle with the pine nuts and serve immediately in warmed bowls.

## Variation
Sometimes I add 4 diced fresh tomatoes to this mixture. You could also add some cooked borlotti beans with chopped parsley.

## Consiglio   **Orecchiette (little ears) from Puglia are a special type of pasta with a chewy texture. You can get them in Italian delis, or use conchiglie instead.**

# Bucatini alle Sarde e Finocchio Bucatini with Sardines and Fennel   serves 4

**This tasty and substantial dish is obviously southern in origin.**

**375g / 13oz bucatini (see page 40)**

**FOR THE SAUCE**
**1 onion, finely chopped**
2 garlic cloves, peeled and crushed
**3 tbsp olive oil**
generous handful of fennel fronds,
finely chopped
**400g / 14oz canned chopped
tomatoes**
I dsp currants
**100g / 3½oz pine nuts**
I tsp dried chilli flakes
**sea salt**
500g / 1lb 2oz fresh sardine
fillets, rinsed

**FOR THE PASTA TOPPING**
**100g / 3½oz fresh breadcrumbs**
2 tbsp olive oil
**4 ripe tomatoes, deseeded and
chopped**
I garlic clove, peeled and crushed
**pinch of dried chilli flakes**
handful of flat-leaf parsley leaves,
chopped

1   First make the sauce: sauté the onion and the garlic in the olive oil. Add the fennel, tomatoes, currants, pine nuts, chilli and a little salt. Simmer, stirring from time to time, for 30 minutes.

2   Add the sardine fillets and cook for 12 minutes – they will break up while cooking.

3   Meanwhile, make the topping: toast the breadcrumbs in a frying pan, mixing in the olive oil, tomatoes, garlic, a little salt and the chilli. Stir constantly, without allowing the breadcrumbs to burn, until they are a nice amber colour and crunchy to the bite. Sprinkle over the parsley.

4   Cook the pasta in a large saucepan of boiling salted water until al dente, i.e. just tender but still firm to the bite.

5   Drain the pasta, reserving a ladleful of the cooking water. Pour half of the sauce into the pan. Add the pasta and stir to coat completely. Pour into a serving dish and cover with the rest of the sauce, adding the reserved cooking water if needed to give enough sauce. Serve immediately with the breadcrumb topping.

## Variation
If you can't get fennel with green fronds attached, add some fresh dill. Although the taste doesn't really compare, if you make this dish with canned sardines, it still makes a very nice supper.

**Consiglio** Instead of squid and peas, you could add chunks of roasted vegetables such as courgettes, peppers or aubergines to the tomato sauce, or Bolognese sauce (page 134) can be used instead of tomato sauce.

# Pasticciata con Calamari e Piselli
## Pasta Pie with Squid and Peas   serves 4–6

This is an excellent supper dish for all the family; children absolutely love it. Most of the ingredients will probably already be in your storecupboard or fridge so more basic versions of it make good 'stand-by' meals – you could, for example, substitute canned tuna for the squid. Pasticciata can be made with or without pastry shells. Naturally here we make it without to keep it light and healthy.

350g/12oz dried conchiglie (see page 42) or rigatoni (see page 41)

about 6 medium squid, prepared

grated zest and juice of 1 unwaxed lemon

200g/7oz fresh peas

2 tbsp dry breadcrumbs

**FOR THE TOMATO SAUCE**

2 tbsp olive oil

1 small onion, finely chopped

400g/14oz canned chopped Italian plum tomatoes

1 tbsp sun-dried tomato paste

handful of mixed herbs (such as sage, thyme, rosemary and parsley), freshly chopped

sea salt and freshly ground black pepper

**FOR THE WHITE SAUCE**

25g/1oz unsalted butter

25g/1oz '00' plain Italian flour or plain flour

600ml/1 pint skimmed milk

1 egg

1  First make the tomato sauce: heat the olive oil in a large saucepan and cook the finely chopped onion over a gentle heat, stirring, until softened. Stir in the tomatoes, then fill the empty can with water and add this to the tomato mixture with the tomato paste and herbs, and salt and pepper to taste. Simmer for 20 minutes.

2  Meanwhile, preheat the oven to 190°C/375°F/Gas 5. Cook the pasta in a large saucepan of boiling salted water until al dente, i.e. just tender but still firm to the bite.

3  Meanwhile, make the white sauce. Melt the butter in a pan, add the flour and cook, stirring, for 1 minute. Add the milk, a little at a time, whisking well after each addition. Bring to the boil and cook, stirring, until the sauce is smooth and thick. Season to taste, then remove the pan from the heat.

4  Chop the squid into rings and sauté in hot oil for about 4 minutes.

5  Drain the cooked pasta and tip it into a baking dish. Add the cooked squid, lemon zest and juice, and the peas to the tomato sauce and adjust its seasoning if necessary. Pour the sauce into the dish and stir well to mix with the pasta.

6  Beat the egg into the white sauce, then pour the sauce over the pasta mixture. Separate the pasta with a fork in several places so that the white sauce fills the gaps. Level the surface, sprinkle with breadcrumbs and bake for 15 minutes until golden brown and bubbly.

# 6
# in anticipo
cook ahead

For busy people or those with large families, it is always useful to be able to make tasty fresh pasta sauces. like traditional Ligurian pesto and its not-so-traditional but equally spirited variations, in advance, when you have the time. Also, when you have just that little bit more time, you can conjure up some of the tasty baked and stuffed pastas, such as lasagne, cannelloni and ravioli. Many of these are actually all the better for being made ahead, as the flavours then get a chance to mingle and develop.

# Mandilli di Seta con Pesto Squares of Pasta with Pesto   serves 2

In Liguria, where this recipe originated, these are called mandilli di seta or 'silk handkerchiefs'. This pesto is the recipe for Italy's classic basil and pine nut sauce. Make it in the summer, when basil is at its most tender, fragrant and prolific. You may like to triple the quantity of pesto and store the extra in a jar for future use. Keep it in the fridge and always ensure that there is enough oil in the jar to cover the pesto, to prevent it from drying out.

**FOR THE PASTA**
**200g/7oz strong white unbleached flour, preferably Italian grade '00'**
pinch of sea salt
**2 large eggs**
I tbsp olive oil

**FOR THE PESTO**
**I garlic clove, crushed**
25g/Ioz pine nuts
**pinch of sea salt**
2 tbsp freshly grated Parmesan cheese, plus extra to serve
**50g/2oz fresh basil leaves**
5 tbsp fruity extra-virgin olive oil

1 Make the pasta dough as described on pages 8–9 and leave to rest in a cool place for about 30 minutes.

2 Roll out the pasta dough in a pasta machine (see pages 10–11). Alternatively, divide the dough into manageable pieces and cover the dough you are not working with. Take each piece of dough and, with the heel of your hand, press it out. Using a long, thin rolling pin and a little flour, gently roll out the dough as thinly as you can. Leave it to dry on a clean tea towel for 30 minutes. Cut the pasta into 15cm/6in squares.

3 Make the pesto: using a pestle and mortar, pound the garlic, pine nuts and salt together. Add the cheese and basil, and continue to pound. Add the oil, a little at a time, and pound until you have a smooth paste.

4 Cook half the pasta squares in boiling salted water for 7 minutes until al dente, i.e. just tender but still firm to the bite. Drain and toss the pasta with some of the sauce, then serve hot with freshly grated Parmesan cheese. Cook and serve the rest in the same way.

## Variations
As they are quite plain, you can also serve these pasta squares with the other pesto ideas that follow, such as Wild Rocket Pesto, Parsley Pesto or Lemon and Mint Pesto (page 112). The walnut sauce for Pansotti (page 116) is also extremely good with them.

# Tortellini con Ricotta Tortellini with Ricotta   serves 6

Because of their unique shape, tortellini are also known in Italy as 'venus navels'. Legend has it that Venus and Jupiter had an assignation one night in an inn, and the chef at the inn peeked through the keyhole of Venus's room to see her lying half-naked on the bed. The sight of her heavenly navel inspired him to rush to the kitchen and create tortellini in its image.

**FOR THE PASTA**
600g / 1lb 5oz strong white unbleached flour, preferably Italian '00' grade
pinch of sea salt
6 large eggs
1 tbsp olive oil
semolina, for sprinkling

**FOR THE FILLING**
150g / 5oz freshly grated Parmesan cheese
150g/5oz ricotta
50g/2oz truffle condiment (see below)
sea salt and freshly ground black pepper

**TO FINISH**
knob of unsalted butter
fresh basil leaves
more freshly grated Parmesan cheese

1 Make the pasta dough as described on pages 8–9 and leave to rest in a cool place for about 30 minutes.

2 Make the filling: mix together the Parmesan cheese, ricotta and truffle condiment, with salt and pepper to taste.

3 Roll out the dough in a pasta machine (see pages 10–11). Alternatively, divide the dough into manageable pieces and keep the dough covered when not being worked. Take one piece of dough and, with the heel of your hand, press it out. Using a long, thin rolling pin and a little flour, gently roll out the pasta to an even sheet, which is almost paper-thin, sprinkling the surface with semolina. Cut the pasta into 10cm/4 in squares.

4 Place a teaspoonful of filling in the centre of each square. Moisten the edges with water then fold one corner over to make a triangle, making sure there is little or no trapped air. Press the edges lightly together, bringing the corners of the triangle in towards another to make a circular shape. Lay the tortellini on baking sheets, sprinkle with semolina and leave to dry for 1 hour.

5 Put the tortellini in a large saucepan of boiling salted water, bring back to the boil, then reduce the heat and poach at a gentle simmer for 4–5 minutes until al dente, i.e. just tender but still firm to the bite. Drain and serve, dressed with a little knob of butter and garnished with basil leaves, with extra Parmesan cheese served separately.

Consiglio **Sprinkling the pasta with semolina as you roll it out helps the pasta to dry and therefore makes it easier to handle.**

**Truffle condiment is a paste of minced truffle, sometimes extended with chopped porcini mushroom to keep the price down. Available from good Italian delis and some supermarkets, it is expensive but a little goes a long way.**

Variations
Other good stuffings for tortellini include blue cheese, and ham and ricotta.

# Pesto di Peperoni Arrostiti con Penne Rigate Roasted Red Pepper Pesto with Penne Rigate  serves 6

Recently there has been an explosion in variations on classic basil pesto in restaurants, but the Italians themselves have been playing with the concept for generations.

500g/1lb 2oz penne rigate (the ridged version of penne, page 39)
fresh basil leaves, to garnish

**FOR THE PESTO**
**4 medium red peppers**
65g/2¼oz ground almonds
**zest of 1 unwaxed lemon, finely chopped**
4 tbsp extra-virgin olive oil, plus a little more to finish
**1 garlic clove, peeled**
2 tsp balsamic vinegar
**50g/2oz freshly grated Parmesan cheese**
sea salt and freshly ground black pepper

1 To make the pesto: preheat the oven to 200°C/400°F/Gas 6. Put the peppers on a baking sheet and roast them in the preheated oven for 25 minutes, turning them once during cooking. They should become charred and deflated. Remove and leave to cool on a wire rack. This can be done a day ahead if that is easier.

2 When the peppers are cool, peel off the skin and remove the seeds. Try to save the precious juices from the peppers by holding them over a bowl as you do this.

3 Put the pepper flesh and juices, and all the other ingredients in the food processor and whiz until blended smooth and thick. Taste and adjust the seasoning if necessary.

4 Cook the pasta in boiling salted water until al dente, i.e. just tender but still firm to the bite. Drain and toss the pasta with the sauce, then garnish with basil leaves to serve.

Consiglio  If you don't want to use the pesto straight away, or just some of it, put it in a sterilized jar (it should fill a 225g/8oz jar) and top with olive oil to act as a preservative. Store in the fridge for up to 2 weeks.

This sauce is not only good with pasta but also makes an excellent salad dressing or can be used to dress freshly steamed vegetables.

**Mint and lemons** Finely chop a generous handful of fresh mint leaves and mix together the finely grated zest of 2 unwaxed lemons and the juice of 3. Replace the peppers, almonds and lemon zest in the basic recipe with this mixture.

**Parsley** Replace the peppers in the basic recipe with a large bunch of flat-leaf parsley, double the amount of lemon zest and replace the almonds with pine nuts. This is also good if you use equal parts parsley and coriander, and both variations are good if you add a deseeded chilli pepper.

**Asparagus** Preheat the oven to 200°C/400°F/Gas 6. Trim a large bunch of asparagus, arrange on a baking sheet, brush lightly with olive oil and season with sea salt. Roast in the preheated oven for 10 minutes, allow to cool and coarsely chop. Use in the basic recipe in place of the peppers and replace the almonds with pine nuts.

**Wild rocket** Wash 2 large bunches of wild rocket well and trim off all the coarse stalks. Use in the basic recipe in place of the peppers and replace the almonds with pine nuts.

# Cannelloni con Fave e Ricotta Cannelloni with Broad Beans and Ricotta   serves 6

**Here the pasta and/or the sauce can be made ahead, or the whole thing can be assembled and kept for a day or two in the fridge before baking – and will actually benefit in terms of flavour.**

**FOR THE PASTA**
150g/5oz Italian grade '00' flour
150g/5oz fine semolina, plus more for sprinkling
pinch of sea salt
2 large free-range eggs
1 tbsp olive oil

**FOR THE FILLING**
1kg/2¼lb broad beans in the pod, podded
350g/12oz ricotta
115g/4oz Pecorino Romano cheese, grated, plus more to serve
1 large garlic clove, crushed
large handful of mint, chopped
sea salt and freshly ground black pepper

**FOR THE BESCIAMELLA SAUCE**
600ml/1 pint milk
2 slices of onion
1 bay leaf
1 blade of mace
3 parsley stalks, bruised
5 whole black peppercorns
50g/2oz butter
45g/1½oz flour
150ml/¼ pint dry white wine

1 To make the pasta, heap the flour and semolina into a mound on the work surface. Sprinkle over the salt and mix well. Hollow out a well in the centre and break in the eggs. Add the olive oil and, with much care and patience, gradually work the eggs and oil into the flour until you have a slab of dough. Shape this into a ball and leave under a towel or in cling film to rest while you prepare the filling.

2 To make the filling, boil or steam the broad beans until tender, about 10 minutes. Drain and leave to cool. Once cool, put half of the beans in a food processor and pulse, leaving some texture. Add the ricotta, Pecorino, garlic and mint, with salt and pepper to taste. Add the remaining whole broad beans and mix well with a wooden spoon.

3 Roll out the pasta dough wafer thin and cut into 8cm/3in squares. Sprinkle lightly with semolina and let dry on a tray for 10–15 minutes.

4 When almost dry, cook the pasta squares in boiling salted water until al dente, i.e. just tender but still firm to the bite. Preheat the oven to 200°C/400°F/Gas 6.

5 To make the besciamella: place the milk in a pan with the onion slices, bay leaf, mace, parsley stalks and peppercorns. Heat over a medium-low heat and bring to a simmer, remove from the heat and leave to infuse for 8–10 minutes.

6 Melt 25g/1oz of butter in a saucepan, stir in the flour and continue stirring over the heat for 1 minute. Remove from the heat, strain in the infused milk and mix well. Return to the heat and stir or whisk continuously until boiling. Add the remaining butter and the wine and simmer for 3 minutes. Season to taste.

7 On each pasta square, spread a tablespoon of the broad bean filling and roll up into a cylinder. Spread half of the besciamella sauce in a casserole or baking dish, place in the filled cannelloni in parallel lines running from the long edge of the dish and cover with the remaining sauce. Sprinkle with the extra grated Pecorino cheese and bake in the oven for 15 minutes. Serve immediately.

## Variation
You can use Bolognese Sauce (page 134) instead of the besciamella.

# Pansotti con Erbe e Formaggi Pansotti with Herbs and Cheese  serves 6–8

In Liguria, the dough for their version of ravioli, pansotti, is flavoured with white wine and the stuffing is made of cheese and *preboggion*, a mixture of many different types of fresh local herbs and wild leaves, like beet, borage, dandelion and wild chicory. The dish is traditionally served with a kind of pesto made from walnuts.

½ **quantity egg pasta (page 8)**
handful of finely chopped parsley, plus some more sprigs for garnish
**very small handful of finely chopped thyme**
flour, for dusting
**50g/2oz unsalted butter**
freshly grated Parmesan cheese, to serve

**FOR THE FILLING**
**250g/9oz ricotta cheese**
150g/5oz freshly grated Parmesan cheese
**large handful of fresh basil leaves, finely chopped**
large handful of flat-leaf parsley, finely chopped
**few sprigs of fresh marjoram or oregano, leaves removed and finely chopped**
I garlic clove, crushed
**I small egg**
sea salt and freshly ground black pepper

**FOR THE WALNUT SAUCE**
**90g/3¼oz shelled fresh walnuts**
I garlic clove
**4 tbsp extra-virgin olive oil**
125ml/4fl oz double cream

1 Make the pasta as described on page 8, but adding the herbs to the well as you mix the ingredients. Leave to rest in a cool place for at least 30 minutes.

2 Make the filling: put the ricotta, Parmesan, herbs, garlic and egg in a bowl, with salt and pepper to taste, and beat well to mix.

3 To make the sauce, put the walnuts, garlic and oil, with salt and pepper to taste, in a food processor and process to a paste, adding up to 125ml/4fl oz warm water to slacken the consistency. Spoon the mixture into a large bowl and add the cream. Beat well to mix, then adjust the seasoning if necessary.

4 Using a pasta machine, roll out one-quarter of the pasta to a 90–100cm/ 36–40in long strip. Cut the strip into two 45–50cm/18–20in lengths (you can do this during rolling if the strip becomes too long to manage).

5 Using a 5cm/2in square ravioli cutter, cut 8–10 squares from one of the pasta strips. Using a teaspoon, put a mound of filling in the centre of each square. Brush a little water around the edge of each square, then fold the square diagonally in half over the filling to make a triangular shape, making sure there is little or no trapped air. Press gently to seal. Spread out the pansotti on a clean floured tea towel, sprinkle lightly with flour and leave to dry while repeating the process with the remaining dough to make 64–80 pansotti altogether.

6 Put the pansotti in a large pan of boiling salted water, bring back to the boil, reduce the heat and poach at a gentle simmer for 4–5 minutes.

7 Meanwhile, put the walnut sauce in a large warmed bowl and add a ladleful of the pasta cooking water to thin it down. Melt the butter in a small saucepan until sizzling. Drain the pansotti and tip them into the bowl of walnut sauce. Drizzle the butter over them. Toss well, then sprinkle with grated Parmesan.

8 Serve immediately, with more grated Parmesan handed around separately.

Consiglio **Both the pansotti and the walnut sauce can be made a day or two ahead and kept in the refrigerator.**

# Culurjones
# Sardinian Ravioli   serves 4–6

**These ravioli, originating from northern Sardinia, can also be served dressed with tomato sauce. The saffron – undoubtedly an inheritance from the days the Moors and Spanish ruled this island – gives them a very distinctive flavour.**

**½ quantity egg pasta (see page 8)**
flour, for dusting
**50g/2oz unsalted butter**
50g/2oz freshly grated Pecorino Sardo cheese

**FOR THE FILLING**
**2 potatoes, each about 200g/7oz, diced**
65g/2¼oz freshly grated Pecorino cheese
**85g/3oz soft fresh Pecorino cheese or soft fresh goats' cheese**
**1 egg yolk**
**large bunch of fresh mint, leaves removed and chopped**
good pinch of saffron powder
**sea salt and freshly ground black pepper**

1 First make the filling: cook the diced potato in salted water for 15 minutes or until soft. Drain the potatoes and tip into a bowl, then mash until smooth. Leave until cold. Add the cheeses, egg yolk, mint and saffron, with salt and pepper to taste and stir well to mix.

2 Using a pasta machine, roll out about one quarter of the pasta into a 90–100cm/36–40in long strip. Cut the strip with a sharp knife into two 45–50cm/18–20in lengths.

3 With a fluted 10cm/4in biscuit cutter, cut out 4–5 discs from one of the pasta strips. Using a heaped teaspoon, put a mound of filling on one side of each disc. Brush a little water around the edge of each disc, then fold the plain side of the disc over the filling to make a half-moon shape, ensuring that there is little or no trapped air. Pleat the curved edge to seal.

4 Put the culurjones on floured clean tea towels, sprinkle with flour and leave to dry. Repeat the process with the remaining dough to make 32–40 culurjones altogether. If you have any stuffing left, re-roll the pasta trimmings and make some more culurjones.

5 Preheat the oven to 190°C/375°F/Gas 5. Put the ravioli in a large saucepan of boiling salted water, bring back to the boil, reduce the heat and poach at a gentle simmer for 4–5 minutes. Meanwhile, melt the butter in a small saucepan.

6 Drain the culurjones, turn them into a large baking dish and pour the melted butter over them and sprinkle with the grated Pecorino. Bake in the oven for 10–15 minutes until golden and bubbling. Allow to stand for 5 minutes before serving.

# Ravioli Fritti Fried Ravioli   serves 6

**Pasta is most often boiled or baked, but deep-frying is another excellent method of cooking it. The pasta becomes a crisp and delicious wrapper around a hot melted-cheese filling, here flavoured with rocket and parsley. The ravioli can be made up to 2 days in advance and stored in the fridge, to be cooked when needed. These make very nice party food, especially if served with a cold tomato sauce as a dip.**

**FOR THE PASTA**
**300g/10½oz strong white unbleached flour or plain white flour**
**pinch of sea salt**
**50g/2oz unsalted butter**
I egg, separated, plus I extra egg yolk
**vegetable oil, for deep-frying**

**FOR THE FILLING**
**115g/4oz Gruyère cheese**
85g/3oz fresh rocket, finely chopped
**40g/1¼oz freshly grated Parmesan cheese**
I egg, beaten
**handful of flat-leaf parsley, finely chopped**
sea salt and freshly ground black pepper

1 To make the pasta, sift the flour and salt on to a work surface. Make a well in the centre. Cut the butter into small dice and add with the egg yolks. Work to a smooth dough, adding a little lukewarm water if necessary.

2 To make the filling, grate the Gruyère cheese and put into a bowl with the rocket, Parmesan, beaten egg, parsley and salt and pepper to taste. Stir well together.

3 Flatten the pasta dough with a rolling pin and roll out into a sheet about 5mm/¼in thick. Cut into 12.5cm/5 in rounds. Divide the filling between the rounds, placing it in the centre of each one. Lightly whisk the egg white. Brush the edges of the round with a little egg white, then fold the pasta over the filling to enclose it completely, ensuring that there is little or no trapped air, and pinch to seal.

4 Heat the oil for deep-frying to 190°C/375°F and drop in the ravioli, a few at a time, and cook until golden brown. Drain on absorbent kitchen paper, while frying the remaining ravioli. Serve hot.

## Variation
These ravioli are also delicious stuffed with Bolognese Sauce (page 134).

# Tortellini con Burro e Salvia Tortellini with Butter and Sage   serves 6

**This Umbrian dish is one of those that I cook regularly as it never disappoints. Sage is yet another ingredient valued by the Italians as it is said to clarify the mind.**

**FOR THE PASTA**
**200g / 7oz strong white unbleached flour, preferably Italian '00' grade, plus more for dusting**
pinch of sea salt
**2 large eggs**
I tbsp olive oil

**FOR THE FILLING**
**100g / 3½oz ricotta**
50g / 2oz Fontina cheese
**50g / 2oz freshly grated Parmesan cheese**
I egg, beaten
**pinch of freshly grated nutmeg**
handful of fresh sage leaves, finely chopped

**TO FINISH**
**50g / 2oz unsalted butter**
handful of fresh sage leaves
**freshly grated Parmesan cheese**

1 Make the pasta dough as described on pages 8–9 and leave to rest in a cool place for about 30 minutes.

2 Mix together all the filling ingredients and beat thoroughly.

3 Roll the dough out in a pasta machine as described on pages 10–11. Alternatively, divide the dough into manageable pieces and keep those you are not working on covered. Take one piece of dough and, with the heel of your hand, press it out. Using a long, thin rolling pin and a little flour, roll out the dough to a paper-thin sheet. Cut the pasta into 5cm / 2in diameter circles. Place small spoonfuls of the filling on one side of each circle, dampen the edges, then fold the dough over the filling to make a half-moon (don't worry, the two edges won't quite meet), making sure there is little or no trapped air, and press down to seal. Curl the triangle around one of your index fingers, bringing the bottom two corners together, and press these together to seal. Leave to dry briefly on a flour-dusted tray.

4 Put the tortellini in a large saucepan of boiling salted water, adding a handful at a time, bring back to the boil, reduce the heat and poach at a gentle simmer for about 3–5 minutes. When they rise to the top of the pan, count 30 seconds, then remove with a slotted spoon and place in a warmed serving dish.

5 Melt the butter and pour over the tortellini. Garnish with sage leaves and serve with a sprinkling of Parmesan cheese.

Consiglio **The tortellini can be prepared in advance and kept in the fridge for up to 2 days.**

## Variation
Try frying the sage leaves until crisp before scattering them over the tortellini.

# Pappardelle with Rabbit Sauce    serves 4

This is a slightly tamer version of the ancient Tuscan classic dish, *pappardelle con lepre* (with hare sauce), generally held to be among the most delicious of all pasta dishes.

25g/1oz dried porcini mushrooms

175ml/6fl oz warm water

1 onion

1 carrot

1 celery stalk

3 bay leaves

25g/1oz unsalted butter

1 tbsp olive oil

50g/2oz pancetta

handful of flat-leaf parsley, roughly chopped, plus more to serve

250g/9oz boneless rabbit meat

6 tbsp dry white wine

200g/7oz can of chopped Italian plum tomatoes

sea salt and freshly ground black pepper

200g/7oz dried pappardelle (see page 58)

1 Put the dried mushrooms in a bowl, pour over the warm water and leave to reconstitute for 10–15 minutes. Finely chop the vegetables, either in a food processor or by hand. Make a tear in the bay leaves to help release their flavour.

2 Heat the butter and oil in a medium saucepan until just sizzling. Add the chopped vegetables, pancetta and parsley, and cook for 5 minutes.

3 Add the rabbit meat and fry on all sides for 3–4 minutes. Pour the wine over and let it reduce for a few minutes, then add the tomatoes. Drain the mushrooms and pour the soaking liquid into the pan. Chop the mushrooms and add them to the mixture with the bay leaves and salt and pepper to taste. Stir well, cover and simmer for 35–45 minutes until the rabbit is tender, stirring occasionally.

4 Remove the pan from the heat and lift out the rabbit pieces with a slotted spoon. Cut them into bite-sized chunks and stir them back into the sauce. Remove and discard the bay leaves. Taste and adjust the seasoning if necessary.

5 Cook the pasta in boiling salted water until al dente, i.e. just tender but still firm to the bite.

6 Reheat the sauce if necessary. Drain the pasta and toss with the sauce in a warmed bowl. Serve immediately, sprinkled with parsley.

Consiglio **This sauce is one that definitely improves in flavour for being made at least a day ahead and then reheated.**

## Spaghetti con Polpettini di Vitello Spaghetti with Veal Meatballs serves 6–8

**This is a classic southern dish that has become a standard in American home cooking.**

350g/12oz dried spaghetti

freshly grated Parmesan cheese, to serve

**FOR THE MEATBALL SAUCE**
350g/12oz minced veal

1 egg

2 tbsp roughly chopped flat-leaf parsley, plus more to serve

sea salt and freshly ground black pepper

1 thick slice of white bread, crusts removed

2 tbsp milk

3 tbsp olive oil

300ml/½ pint passata

400ml/14fl oz vegetable stock

1 tsp sugar

1 Make the meatballs: put the veal in a large bowl, add the egg and half of the parsley, and season with salt and pepper. Tear the bread into small pieces and place in a small bowl. Moisten with the milk, leave to soak for a few minutes. Squeeze out the excess milk and crumble the bread over the meat mixture. Mix everything together with a wooden spoon, then use your hands to squeeze and knead the mixture so that it becomes smooth and sticky.

2 Wash your hands, rinse them under cold running water, then pick up small pieces of the mixture and roll them between the palms of your hands to make about 40–60 small balls. Place the meatballs on a tray and chill for 30 minutes.

3 Heat the oil in a large frying pan and cook the meatballs in batches until browned on all sides.

4 Pour the passata and stock into a large saucepan, heat gently, then add the sugar, with salt and pepper to taste. Add the meatballs, then bring to the boil. Lower the heat, cover and simmer for 20 minutes.

5 Cook the pasta in boiling salted water until al dente, i.e. just tender but still firm to the bite.

6 Drain the pasta and tip it into a warmed large bowl. Pour the sauce over the pasta and toss gently. Sprinkle with the remaining parsley and serve with Parmesan cheese.

# Ravioli alla Romagnola Ravioli with Pork and Turkey   serves 6–8

**This Roman-style ravioli, stuffed with minced meat and cheese and scented with fresh herbs, makes an absolutely delicious dish.**

½ **quantity egg pasta (see page 8)**
flour, for dusting
**50g/2oz butter**
large bunch of fresh sage, leaves removed and roughly chopped, plus more to serve
**4 tbsp freshly grated Parmesan cheese, plus more to serve**

**FOR THE FILLING**
**25g/1oz butter**
150g/5oz minced pork
**115g/4oz minced turkey**
4 fresh sage leaves, finely chopped
**sprig of rosemary, leaves removed and finely chopped**
sea salt and freshly ground black pepper
**2 tbsp dry white wine**
65g/2¼oz ricotta cheese
**3 tbsp grated Parmesan cheese**
1 egg
**freshly grated nutmeg**

1 To make the filling: melt the butter in a medium saucepan, add the minced pork and turkey with the herbs and cook gently for 5–6 minutes, stirring frequently and breaking up any lumps in the meat with a wooden spoon. Add salt and pepper to taste and stir well to mix thoroughly.

2 Add the wine to the pan and stir again. Simmer for 1–2 minutes until reduced slightly, then cover the pan and simmer gently for about 20 minutes, stirring occasionally. With a slotted spoon, transfer the meat to a bowl and leave to cool.

3 Add the ricotta and Parmesan cheeses to the bowl of meat, together with the egg and freshly grated nutmeg to taste. Stir well to mix the ingredients thoroughly.

4 Using a pasta machine, roll out one-quarter of the pasta dough into a 90–100cm/36–40in long strip. Cut the strip with a sharp knife into two 45–50cm/18–20inch lengths (you can do this during rolling if the strips become too long to manage).

5 Using a teaspoon, put 10–12 little mounds of the filling along one side of one of the pasta strips, spacing them evenly. Brush a little water on to the pasta strip around each mound, then fold the plain side of the pasta strip over the filling. Starting from the folded edge, press down gently with your fingertip around each mound of filling, pushing the air out at the unfolded edge. Sprinkle lightly with flour.

6 With a fluted pasta wheel, cut along each long side in between each mound to make small square shapes. Dust lightly with flour. Put the ravioli in a single layer on floured clean tea towels and leave to dry while repeating the process with the remaining pasta to make 80–96 ravioli altogether.

7 Drop the ravioli into a large pan of salted boiling water, bring back to the boil, reduce the heat and poach at a gentle simmer for 4–5 minutes. Meanwhile, melt the butter in a small pan.

8 Remove the ravioli with a slotted spoon as they are cooked and serve dressed with the melted butter, herbs and cheese.

# Lasagne alla Bolognese Lasagne Bolognese   serves 6

This is the classic lasagne, based on a rich, meaty filling, as you would expect from an authentic bolognese recipe.

**1 quantity Bolognese Sauce (page 134)**
1 quantity Besciamella sauce (page 129)
150–250ml/5–9fl oz hot beef stock
12 no-need-to-precook dried lasagne sheets
50g/2oz freshly grated Parmesan cheese

1 Preheat the oven to 190°C/375°F/Gas 5. If the sauces are cold, reheat them. Once hot, stir enough stock into the Bolognese Sauce to make it quite runny.

2 Spread about a third of the Bolognese over the bottom of a baking dish. Cover this with about one-quarter of the white sauce, followed by 4 sheets of lasagne. Repeat the layers twice more, then cover the top layer of lasagne with the remaining white sauce and sprinkle the grated Parmesan evenly over the top.

3 Bake for 40 minutes, until the pasta feels tender when pierced with a skewer. Allow to stand for about 10 minutes before serving.

Consiglio  **The Bolognese Sauce can be made up to 3 days in advance and kept in a covered container in the fridge.**

**To reheat leftover lasagne, prick it all over with a skewer, then slowly pour a little milk on top to moisten. Cover with foil and place in the oven preheated to 190°C/375°F/Gas 5 for 20 minutes or until bubbling.**

**Do not reheat lasagne if the meat sauce was made in advance, as it can be dangerous to reheat meat dishes more than once.**

## Variations
Make a meatless version using a spicy tomato sauce (see page 105, adding some crushed dried chilli flakes to taste) instead of the Bolognese. Alternatively, omit the Bolognese and layer in some fresh spinach and sun-dried tomatoes.

Consiglio  **Using Italian 00 flour produces a lighter white sauce.**

# Lasagne con Polpettini Lasagne with Meatballs   serves 6–8

275g/11oz minced beef
275g/11oz minced pork
1 large egg
50g/2oz fresh white breadcrumbs
5 tbsp freshly grated Parmesan cheese
2 tbsp chopped fresh flat-leaf parsley
2 garlic cloves, crushed
sea salt and freshly ground black pepper
4 tbsp olive oil
1 onion, finely chopped
1 carrot, finely chopped
1 celery stalk, finely chopped
2 x 400g/14oz cans of chopped Italian plum tomatoes
2 tsp finely chopped fresh oregano or basil
6–8 no-need-to-precook dried lasagne sheets

FOR THE BESCIAMELLA SAUCE
700ml/1¼ pints milk
1 bay leaf
1 fresh thyme sprig
50g/2oz unsalted butter
50g/2oz Italian grade '00' flour or plain flour
freshly grated nutmeg

1 First make the meatballs; put 175g/6oz each of the minced beef and pork in a large bowl. Add the egg, breadcrumbs, 2 tablespoons of the grated Parmesan, half the parsley, half the garlic and plenty of salt and pepper. Mix everything together with a wooden spoon, then use your hands to squeeze and knead the mixture so that it becomes smooth and quite sticky.

2 Wash your hands, rinse them under cold running water, then pick up small pieces of the mixture and roll between your palms to make about 30 walnut-sized balls. Place on a tray and chill for about 30 minutes.

3 Meanwhile, put the milk for the besciamella sauce in a saucepan. Make a tear in the bay leaf, then add it and the thyme sprig to the milk and bring to the boil. Remove from the heat, cover and leave to infuse.

4 Make the meat sauce: heat half the oil in a medium pan, add the onion, carrot, celery and remaining garlic, and stir over a low heat for 5 minutes or so until softened. Add the remaining minced meats and cook gently for 10 minutes, stirring frequently and breaking up any lumps. Stir in salt and pepper to taste, then add the tomatoes, remaining parsley and the oregano or basil. Stir well, cover and simmer gently for 45–60 minutes, stirring occasionally.

5 Meanwhile, heat the remaining oil in a large nonstick frying pan. When hot, cook the meatballs in batches over a medium-to-high heat for 5–8 minutes until browned all over. Shake the pan from time to time so that the meatballs roll around. As they cook, transfer them to kitchen paper to drain.

6 Preheat the oven to 190°C/375°F/Gas 5. Make the besciamella sauce: strain the milk to remove the bay and thyme. Melt the butter in a medium pan, add the flour and cook, stirring, for 1–2 minutes. Add the milk, a little at a time, whisking vigorously after each addition. Bring to the boil and cook, stirring constantly, until thick and smooth. Grate in a little nutmeg to taste and season with salt and pepper. Whisk well, then remove from the heat.

7 Spread about one-third of the meat sauce in the bottom of a large shallow baking dish. Add half of the meatballs, then spread with one-third of the besciamella and cover with half the lasagne sheets. Repeat these layers, then top with the remaining meat sauce and besciamella. Sprinkle the remaining grated Parmesan evenly over the surface.

8 Bake for 30–40 minutes or until golden brown and bubbling. Allow to stand for 10 minutes before serving. If you like, garnish each serving with parsley.

# impressionante

Pasta has become so much a part of everyday family eating in this country that people often look askance at me when I suggest serving it at dinner parties or for special occasions. Nevertheless, pasta can be rich and luxurious, and every bit as impressive as a roast or an elaborate layered chef's extravaganza. Certain ingredients immediately endow pasta with that touch of class — crab and lobster in fillings for stuffed pasta, say, or saffron to colour the pasta. Some techniques do it, like open layered lasagne (Vincisgrassi Aperto) or stuffed rolls of pasta, sliced and grilled (Rotolo Ripieno). Essentially, however, the dishes remain simple, and it is the shape of the pasta and dramatic or unusual presentation that do the job.

# Agnolotti con Taleggio e Maggiorana Agnolotti with Taleggio and Marjoram   serves 6 as a starter, 4 as a main course

**The filling for these little half-moons is simple, but the combination is very effective.**

½ quantity fresh egg pasta (page 8)

350g / 12oz Taleggio cheese

**about 2 tbsp finely chopped marjoram, plus extra to garnish**

sea salt and freshly ground black pepper

**flour, for dusting**

115g / 4oz unsalted butter

**freshly grated Parmesan cheese, to serve**

1 Using a pasta machine, roll out a quarter of the pasta into a 90–100cm / 36–40in strip. Cut the strip with a sharp knife into two 45–50cm / 18–20in lengths.

2 Cut 8–10 little cubes of Taleggio and place them along one side of one of the pasta strips, spacing them evenly. Sprinkle each Taleggio cube with a little chopped marjoram and pepper to taste. Brush a little water around each cube of cheese then fold the plain side of the pasta strip over them. Starting from the folded edge, press down gently with your fingertip around each cube, pushing the air out at the unfolded edge. Sprinkle lightly with flour.

3 Using only half of a 5cm / 2in fluted round biscuit cutter, cut the pasta around each cube of cheese to make a half-moon shape. The folded edge should be the straight edge. If you like, press the cut edges of the agnolotti with the tines of a fork to give a decorative effect. Put the agnolotti on floured clean tea towels, sprinkle lightly with flour and leave to dry while repeating the process with the remaining pasta, cheese, marjoram and pepper to make between 64 and 80 agnolotti in total.

4 Drop the agnolotti into a large saucepan of boiling salted water, bring back to the boil, reduce the heat and poach at a gentle simmer for 4–5 minutes until al dente, i.e. just tender but still firm to the bite

5 Meanwhile, melt the butter in a small saucepan. Drain the agnolotti and divide them equally among 6 or 8 warmed large bowls. Drizzle the sizzling butter over them and serve immediately, sprinkled with freshly grated Parmesan and chopped fresh marjoram. Hand round more grated Parmesan separately.

Consiglio **Marjoram is traditional with the Taleggio cheese in this recipe, both for the filling and the sizzling butter, but you can use other fresh herbs, such as sage, basil or flat-leaf parsley.**

# Tagliarini al Tartufo Bianco Tagliarini with White Truffle    serves 4

There is nothing quite like the fragrance and flavour of the white truffle. It is one of the rarest and, therefore, most expensive of truffles, and comes from around the town of Alba in Piedmont. This simple style of serving it is one of the best ways to enjoy it. Tagliarini, or tagliolini, is like a thinner tagliatelle.

**350g/12oz fresh or dried tagliarini (see above)**

sea salt and freshly ground black pepper

**75g/3oz unsalted butter, diced**

4 tbsp freshly grated Parmesan cheese

**1 tsp freshly grated nutmeg**

1 small white truffle (about 25g/1oz)

1 Cook the pasta in boiling salted water until al dente, i.e. just tender but still firm to the bite.

2 Drain the cooked pasta thoroughly and tip it into a warmed large bowl. Add the diced butter, grated Parmesan cheese, freshly grated nutmeg and a little salt and pepper to taste. Toss until the pasta is well coated.

3 Divide the pasta equally among 4 warmed bowls and shave paper-thin slivers of the white truffle on top. Serve immediately.

Consiglio  **White truffles can be bought during the months of September and October.**

# Pappardelle con Tartufi e Porcini Pappardelle with Truffles and Porcini    serves 2

**50g/2oz dried sliced porcini**

200g/7oz pappardelle (long broad pasta, see page 58)

**sea salt and freshly ground black pepper**

1 tbsp olive oil

**1 garlic clove, crushed**

50g/2oz truffle condiment (see page 109)

**2 tbsp mascarpone cheese**

1 tbsp dry white wine

**shavings of Parmesan cheese, to serve**

1 Soak the dried porcini in cold water to cover for 20 minutes, then drain (you can strain the soaking water into the pasta water or use it too slacken the sauce if you like).

2 Cook the pasta in boiling salted water until al dente, i.e. just tender but still firm to the bite, about 12 minutes.

3 Meanwhile, heat the oil in a pan, add the garlic, truffle condiment and porcini, and cook gently for 10 minutes. Add the mascarpone cheese and wine, with salt and pepper to taste.

4 Drain the cooked pasta and toss in the truffle and porcini mixture. Serve scattered with the Parmesan shavings.

# Cappellacci alla Bolognese Cheese Cappellacci with Bolognese Sauce serves 6–8 generously

In Emilia-Romagna it is traditional to serve these cappellacci with a rich meat sauce but, if you prefer, you can serve them with a tomato sauce or just melted butter.

1/2 quantity of fresh egg pasta (page 8)

flour, for dusting

2 litres / 3 1/2 pt beef stock (page 31)

freshly grated Parmesan cheese, to serve

basil leaves, to garnish

**FOR THE FILLING**

250g / 9oz ricotta cheese

85g / 3oz Taleggio cheese, rind removed and diced very small

4 tbsp freshly grated Parmesan cheese

1 small egg

freshly grated nutmeg

sea salt and freshly ground black pepper

**FOR THE BOLOGNESE SAUCE**

25g / 1oz butter

1 tbsp olive oil

1 onion, finely chopped

2 carrots, finely chopped

2 celery stalks, finely chopped

2 garlic cloves, finely chopped

115g / 4oz pancetta, cut into small cubes

250g / 9oz lean minced pork

250g / 9oz lean minced beef

125ml / 4fl oz dry white wine

2 x 400g / 14oz cans of chopped Italian plum tomatoes

450–750ml / 16–26fl oz beef stock

100ml / 3 1/2 fl oz double cream

1 To make the filling: put the ricotta, Taleggio and grated Parmesan cheese in a bowl and mash together with a fork. Add the egg and freshly grated nutmeg with salt and pepper to taste, and stir well to mix.

2 Using a pasta machine, roll out one-quarter of the pasta into a 90 x 100cm / 36 x 40in strip. Cut the strip with a sharp knife into 45–50cm / 18–20in lengths. Using a 6–7.5cm / 2 1/2–3in square ravioli cutter, cut 6 or 7 squares from one of the pasta strips. Using a teaspoon, put a mound of filling in the centre of each square. Brush a little water around the edge of each square, then fold the square diagonally in half over the filling to make a triangular shape. Press to seal. Wrap the triangle around one of your index fingers, bringing the bottom two corners together. Pinch the ends together to seal, then press with your fingertips around the top edge of the filling to make an indentation so that the 'hat' looks like a bishop's mitre. Put the cappellacci on floured clean tea towels, sprinkle with flour and leave to dry while repeating the process with the remaining dough to make 48–56 cappellacci in total.

3 To make the Bolognese Sauce: heat the butter and oil in a large saucepan until sizzling. Add the vegetables, garlic and pancetta, and cook over a medium heat, stirring frequently, for 10 minutes or until the vegetables have softened. Add the meats, lower the heat and cook gently for 10 minutes, stirring frequently and breaking up any lumps in the meat with a wooden spoon. Stir in salt and pepper to taste, then add the wine and stir again. Simmer for about 5 minutes or until reduced.

4 Add the tomatoes and 250ml / 9fl oz of the stock, and bring to the boil. Stir well then lower the heat, half cover the pan with a lid and leave to simmer very gently for 2 hours. Stir occasionally during this time and add more stock as it becomes absorbed.

5 Add the cream to the meat sauce. Stir well to mix, then simmer the sauce for another 30 minutes, stirring frequently.

6 Bring the stock for cooking the pasta to the boil in a large saucepan, drop the cappellacci into it, bring back to the boil, reduce the heat and poach at a gentle simmer for 4–5 minutes. Drain the cappellacci and divide them among 6–8 warmed bowls. Spoon the hot Bolognese Sauce over the cappellacci and sprinkle with grated Parmesan and basil leaves. Serve immediately.

# Rotolo Ripieno Spinach, Ricotta and Tomato Pasta Roll   serves 4

**I first enjoyed this pasta dish while holidaying in Umbria. I was so impressed with the unique way of grilling the pasta to give it a crunchy outer texture and the stylish presentation that I begged for the recipe. Eventually after fraternizing the restaurant on five consecutive days, the chef relented to my entreaties, so here is the recipe for you to enjoy too.**

**½ quantity of egg pasta (see page 8)**
25g/1oz unsalted butter, melted, plus more for greasing
**50g/2oz freshly grated Parmesan cheese**

**FOR THE FILLING**
**4 plum tomatoes**
350g/12oz fresh spinach
**175g/6oz ricotta**
freshly grated nutmeg
**sea salt and freshly grated black pepper**
50g/2oz freshly grated Parmesan cheese

1 Make the pasta as described on page 8.

2 Start preparing the filling: put the tomatoes in a bowl, cover with boiling water for about 40 seconds, then plunge them into cold water. Skin and chop the flesh.

3 Put the spinach in a saucepan with only the water still clinging to the leaves after washing. Cook for about 5 minutes over a medium-high heat. Drain the spinach well, squeezing out as much excess water as you can.

4 Finely chop the drained spinach and put it in a bowl. Add the tomatoes and ricotta, with nutmeg, salt and pepper to taste, and mix together with the Parmesan cheese.

5 Roll the pasta dough out to a rectangular sheet about 3mm/⅛in thick. Place it on a large piece of muslin and spread the filling over the dough, leaving a 3cm/1¼in border clear around the edge. By lifting one end of the muslin, roll up the dough like a Swiss roll. Wrap it in the muslin and secure the ends with string like a Christmas cracker.

6 Place the roll in a long, narrow flameproof casserole, roasting tin or fish kettle and cover with lightly salted cold water. Bring to the boil and simmer for 30 minutes. Remove from the water and leave to cool for 5 minutes. Preheat a hot grill.

7 Remove the muslin and cut the roll into slices about 2cm/¾in thick. Place these side by side, or slightly overlapping, in a buttered heatproof dish. Pour the melted butter over the slices, sprinkle them with the Parmesan and grill for 5 minutes until golden. Serve immediately, straight from the dish or on serving plates, sprinkled with a little black pepper and more melted butter or extra-virgin olive oil.

Consiglio The pasta roll can be made in advance and kept in the fridge for up to 2 days. First, allow it to return to room temperature, then slice and grill as above. Also, leftover pasta can be used like pastry, to line, say, a pie or quiche dish.

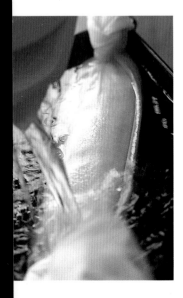

# Garganelli con Asparagi e Panna Garganelli with Asparagus and Cream   serves 4

**A speciality of Romagna, garganelli are made from little squares of pasta rolled into quill shapes and then grooved.**

**bunch of fresh young asparagus (about 250–350g/9–12oz)**
sea salt and freshly ground black pepper
**350g/12oz dried garganelli (see above)**
25g/1oz unsalted butter
**200ml/7fl oz double cream**
2 tbsp dry white wine
**85–115g/3–4oz freshly grated Parmesan cheese**
2 tbsp chopped mixed fresh herbs, such as basil, flat-leaf parsley, marjoram and oregano

1 Trim off and throw away the woody end of the asparagus (after trimming you should have about 200g/7oz of asparagus spears). Cut the spears at an angle into pieces that are roughly the same length and shape as the garganelli.

2 Reserving the tips, blanch the asparagus spears in boiling salted water for 2 minutes, adding the tips for the second minute only. Immediately drain the asparagus spears and tips, rinse in cold water and set aside.

3 Cook the pasta in boiling salted water until al dente, i.e. just tender but still firm to the bite.

4 Meanwhile, put the butter and cream in a medium saucepan, add salt and pepper to taste and bring to the boil. Simmer for a few minutes until the cream reduces slightly and thickens. Add the asparagus, wine and about half the grated Parmesan. Taste and adjust the seasoning if necessary. Keep on a low heat.

5 Drain the cooked pasta and tip it into a warm bowl. Pour over the sauce, sprinkle with herbs and toss well. Serve topped with the remaining Parmesan.

# Tagliatelle con Radicchio e Panna Tagliatelle with Radicchio and Cream   serves 4

**I recommend tasty long, thin radicchio di Treviso for this recipe but radicchio rotondo works just as well.**

**225g/8oz dried tagliatelle**
sea salt and freshly ground black pepper
**85g/3oz pancetta or bacon, diced**
25g/1oz unsalted butter
**1 onion, finely chopped**
115–175g/4–6oz radicchio, shredded
**1 garlic clove, finely chopped**
150ml/¼ pint double cream
**50g/2oz grated Parmesan cheese**
handful of flat-leaf parsley, chopped

1 Cook the pasta in boiling salted water until al dente, i.e. just tender but still firm to the bite.

2 Meanwhile, gently heat the pancetta or bacon in a pan until the fat runs. Increase the heat and stir-fry for 5 minutes. Add the butter, onion and radicchio, and stir-fry for 4 minutes. Add the garlic and stir-fry for 1 minute more, until the onion is lightly coloured. Pour in the cream and add the Parmesan with seasoning to taste. Stir-fry for 1–2 minutes until bubbling. Adjust the seasoning.

3 Drain pasta, tip into a bowl, pour over sauce and toss well with the parsley.

# Cannelloni allo Zafferano Cannelloni with Saffron Sauce   serves 2

This northern dish is perfect for entertaining as it can be made ahead of time. The delicious cheesy artichoke filling and the elegant mascarpone and saffron sauce never fail to impress.

**4 sheets of lasagne, each about 16 x 12.5cm / 6½ x 5 in**
sea salt and freshly ground black pepper

**FOR THE FILLING**
**2 tbsp olive oil**
1 small onion, chopped
**4 canned artichoke hearts, drained, rinsed and chopped**
50g / 2oz mozzarella cheese, chopped
**115g / 4oz ricotta cheese**
50g / 2oz Dolcelatte cheese
**1 tsp finely chopped fresh rosemary**

**FOR THE SAUCE**
**15g / ½oz unsalted butter**
½ garlic clove, crushed
**large pinch of saffron strands**
1 tbsp white wine
**125g / 4oz mascarpone cheese**
sea salt and freshly ground black pepper

1 Preheat the oven to 180°C / 350°F / Gas 4. Put the pasta in a large saucepan of boiling salted water and bring back to the boil. Boil for 1–2 minutes, then drain and rinse under cold water.

2 To make the filling, heat the oil in a saucepan, add the onion and fry until soft. Add the chopped artichokes and cook for 5 minutes. Add the mozzarella, ricotta, Dolcelatte cheese and rosemary. Season well with salt and pepper and mix well together.

3 To make the sauce, melt the butter in a saucepan, add the garlic and saffron and heat gently. Add the wine and mascarpone cheese, with salt and pepper to taste, and simmer for 5 minutes.

4 To assemble the dish, place some filling down the centre of each pasta sheet. Moisten the edges with water and roll each rectangle up from one of its narrow edges to form a thick tube. Arrange the cannelloni in a greased ovenproof dish, pour the sauce over and cover with foil.

5 Bake in the oven for 20 minutes, then serve immediately.

Consiglio   **For best results, prepare the sauce the day before you are going to serve it, to allow the flavours to mature.**

## Variation
The saffron sauce will also give a touch of elegance to cappellacci stuffed with a Bolognese sauce (page 134) or cannelloni with a broad bean filling (page 114).

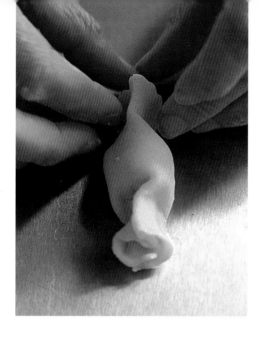

# Bonbons con Funghi di Bosco e Ricotta Bonbons filled with Wild Mushrooms and Ricotta  serves 6 as a starter or 4 as a main course

**These bonbons are best made with thinly rolled homemade pasta, as per the recipe on page 8 but using only 200g/7oz of each flour and 4 eggs.**

**6 sheets of fresh egg pasta (see above), about 28 x 24 cm / 11 x 9½in**

I egg, lightly beaten

**FOR THE FILLING**

**200g/7oz wild mushrooms, finely chopped**

150g/5oz flat mushrooms, finely chopped

**½ onion, grated**

150g/5oz ricotta cheese

**2 tbsp freshly grated Parmesan cheese**

½ tsp finely chopped fresh sage

**½ tsp finely chopped fresh oregano**

½ tsp finely chopped fresh parsley

**pinch of freshly grated nutmeg**

freshly ground black pepper

**TO FINISH**

**single cream or melted butter, for coating**

freshly grated Parmesan cheese

1 Cut each pasta sheet into 9 rectangles, each about 7.5 x 5 cm / 3 x 2 in. Using a scalloped pastry wheel, trim the shorter ends of each rectangle.

2 Mix all the filling ingredients together. Place a teaspoon of filling in the centre of each pasta rectangle. Brush the beaten egg down one long side and fold the pasta to form a tube. Press to seal, trying to remove as much trapped air as possible, then pinch and twist the ends tightly, like a bonbon wrapper. As each bonbon is made, set it aside, uncovered, to rest.

3 Drop the bonbons, a few at a time, into a large saucepan of boiling salted water, bring back to the boil, reduce the heat and then poach at a gentle simmer for 4–5 minutes or until just tender. Remove with a slotted spoon and pile into a warmed serving dish.

4 Toss in cream or butter and sprinkle with Parmesan cheese to serve.

## Variation

These bonbons also suit a herb or spinach and ricotta stuffing (see pages 116 and 137).

# Ravioli al Granchio Ravioli with Crab   serves 4

**I first enjoyed this ravioli with crab at Venice – indisputably the home of the finest crab in Italy. It makes a super dinner party dish and is relatively straightforward.**

**½ quantity of fresh egg pasta
(page 8)**
**flour, for dusting**
**90g/3¼oz unsalted butter**
**juice of 1 lemon**

**FOR THE FILLING**
**175g/6oz mascarpone cheese**
**175g/6oz crab meat**
**handful of finely chopped fresh
flat-leaf parsley**
**finely grated zest of 1 unwaxed
lemon**
**sea salt and freshly ground black
pepper**

1 First make the filling: put the mascarpone in a bowl, mash well with a fork and add the crab meat, parsley and lemon zest with salt and pepper to taste. Stir well.

2 Using a pasta machine, roll out one-quarter of the pasta into a 90–100cm/36–40in strip. With a sharp knife, cut the strip into four 45–50cm/18–20in lengths (you can do this during the rolling if the strip gets too long to manage). Using a 6cm/2½in fluted biscuit cutter, cut out 8 discs from each pasta strip.

3 Using a teaspoon, put a mound of filling in the centre of half the discs. Brush a little water around the edge of the filled discs, then top each with another disc and press the edges to seal, trying to eliminate as much trapped air as you can. For a decorative finish, press the edges with the tines of a fork.

4 Put the ravioli on a floured dish, sprinkle lightly with flour and leave to dry while repeating the process with the remaining dough and filling to make 32 ravioli in all.

5 Add the ravioli to a large saucepan of boiling salted water, bring back to the boil, reduce the heat and then poach at a gentle simmer for 4–5 minutes.

6 Meanwhile, melt the butter with the lemon juice until sizzling. Drain the ravioli and divide them equally among 4 warmed bowls. Drizzle the lemon butter over the ravioli and serve immediately.

Consiglio **You can use all white crab meat or a mixture of white and dark. If you use dark meat, the flavour will obviously be much stronger.**

**lobster and herbs** Bring a large pot of heavily salted water with 2 fresh bay leaves in it to a rapid boil and drop a whole live lobster into it (the RSPCA recommended way). Cook for 20 minutes, then remove from the water and leave to cool. Crack open the lobster and its claws and remove all the meat. Use this instead of the crab meat. If there is more than you need, use it in a salad.

## spinach and ricotta
In a tightly closed pan, cook 450g/1lb young spinach leaves in just the water that clings to their leaves after washing for a few minutes only, then squeeze out as much water as possible from them (between two matching plates). Chop roughly and mix 125g/4oz ricotta, some seasoning and perhaps a little lemon juice and some freshly grated nutmeg.

## walnut, ricotta and basil
Chop 200g/7oz shelled weight of walnuts and a good handful of basil leaves. Mix well with 125g/4oz of ricotta, the finely grated zest of a lemon, 2 finely chopped garlic cloves and seasoning to taste.

## pumpkin, sage and ricotta
Cook 450g/1lb peeled and chopped pumpkin until tender, then mash with 125g/4oz ricotta, and mix in a handful of chopped fresh sage leaves, 85g/3oz grated Parmesan cheese and plenty of seasoning.

# Tagliatelle con Capesanti Tagliatelle with Scallops  serves 4

**200g/7oz scallops, each sliced across into 2 discs**

**2 tbsp plain flour**

**sea salt and freshly ground black pepper**

**45g/1½oz unsalted butter**

**1 small onion, finely chopped**

**1 small fresh red chilli, deseeded and very finely chopped**

**2 tbsp finely chopped fresh flat-leaf parsley**

**4 tbsp brandy**

**7 tbsp fish stock**

**350g/12oz tagliatelle**

1 Toss the scallops in the flour, then shake off the excess. Bring a saucepan of salted water to the boil ready for cooking the pasta.

2 Meanwhile, melt the butter in a saucepan. Add the onion, chilli and half the parsley, and fry over a medium heat, stirring frequently, for 1–2 minutes. Add the scallops and toss over the heat for 1–2 minutes.

3 Pour the brandy over the scallops and immediately (and carefully) set it alight with a match. As soon as the flames have died down, stir in the fish stock, with salt and pepper to taste. Mix well, simmer for 2–3 minutes, then cover the pan and remove it from the heat.

4 Add the pasta to the boiling water and cook it until al dente, i.e. just tender but still firm to the bite.

5 Drain the pasta, add to the sauce and toss over a medium heat until mixed. Serve at once, sprinkling over the remaining parsley.

Consiglio **Buy fresh scallops with their coral if possible. They always have a better texture and flavour than frozen scallops, which will always be very watery. Diver-caught scallops are better than the more common dredged ones – you can usually tell the latter as their shells are more likely to be scraped and damaged.**

# Chiaroscuro Squid Ink Pasta with Ricotta and Scallops  serves 4

Versions of this very dramatic-looking dish are served in smart restaurants in Italy. I have added some tiny queen scallops to make it even more of a special-occasion treat. Obviously the Italian name comes from the word for the treatment of light and shade in a painting.

**350g / 12oz fresh or dried spaghetti nero (squid ink pasta, pages 8–12)**
sea salt and freshly ground black pepper
**4 tbsp ricotta cheese (as fresh as possible)**
4 tbsp extra-virgin olive oil
**about 20 little queen scallops**
1 small fresh red chilli, deseeded and finely chopped
**small handful of fresh basil leaves**

1 Cook the pasta in boiling salted water until al dente, i.e. just tender but still firm to the bite.

2 Meanwhile, put the ricotta in a bowl, add salt and pepper to taste and use a little of the hot water from the pasta pan to mix it to a smooth cream consistency. Taste and adjust the seasoning again.

3 Heat a little of the oil in a large frying pan and, when it is quite hot, sear the scallops for no more than a minute on each side. Season, remove from the heat and keep warm.

4 Drain the cooked pasta and rinse out the pan. Heat the rest of the oil gently in the clean pan and add the pasta with the chilli and salt and pepper to taste. Toss quickly over a high heat to combine.

5 Divide the pasta equally among 4 warmed bowls, then top with the ricotta. Sprinkle with the cooked scallops and then the basil leaves, and serve immediately.

# Garganelli con Salmone e Gamberi Garganelli with Salmon and Prawns   **serves 4**

**350g/12oz salmon fillets**

**200ml/7fl oz dry white wine**

**a few basil leaves, plus more to garnish**

sea salt and freshly ground black pepper

**150ml/¼ pint double cream**

6 ripe plum tomatoes, skinned and finely chopped

**350g/12oz garganelli (see page 138)**

115g/4oz peeled cooked prawns

1 Put the salmon in a wide shallow pan, skin side up. Pour over the wine, scatter in the basil and sprinkle with salt and pepper. Bring to the boil, cover and simmer gently for no more than 5 minutes. Using a fish slice, lift the fish out and set aside to cool slightly.

2 Add the cream and tomatoes to the liquid remaining in the pan and bring to the boil. Stir well, lower the heat and simmer, uncovered, for 10–15 minutes until it thickens slightly.

3 Meanwhile, cook the pasta in a large saucepan of boiling salted water until al dente, i.e. just tender but still firm to the bite.

4 When cool enough to handle, flake the fish into large chunks, carefully discarding the skin and any bones. Add the fish to the sauce, together with the prawns, shaking the pan until the fish and shellfish are well coated. Taste and adjust the seasoning.

5 Drain the cooked pasta and tip it into a warmed serving bowl. Spoon the sauce over the pasta and toss well to combine. Serve immediately, garnished with more basil leaves.

## Variations

Instead of the salmon you can use any firm white fish, such as cod or haddock, or lobster meat left over from the recipe on page 144. I have cooked this using sea bass and it was quite delicious.

# Tagliolini Neri con Vongole e Cozze Squid Ink Tagliolini with Clams and Mussels   serves 6 as a starter, 4 as a main course

**Served in a white china bowl, this makes a stunning dish for a dinner party.**

450g / 1lb fresh mussels
450g / 1lb fresh clams
4 tbsp olive oil
1 small onion, finely chopped
2 garlic cloves, finely chopped
large handful of fresh flat-leaf parsley, plus more to garnish
sea salt and freshly ground black pepper
175ml / 6fl oz dry white wine
250ml / 9fl oz fish stock
1 small fresh red chilli, deseeded and chopped
350g / 12oz tagliolini or tagliarini (page 133) nero (squid ink pasta)

1 Scrub the mussels and clams under cold running water and discard any that are damaged or that are open and do not close when sharply tapped against the work surface.

2 Heat the half the oil in a large saucepan, add the onion and cook gently for about 5 minutes until softened. Sprinkle in the garlic, then add about half the parsley sprigs, with salt and pepper to taste. Add the mussels and clams, and pour in the wine. Cover with the lid and bring to the boil over a high heat. Cook for about 5 minutes, shaking the pan frequently, until the shellfish have opened.

3 Tip the mussels and clams into a fine sieve set over a bowl and let the liquid drain through. Discard the aromatics in the sieve, together with any mussels or clams that have failed to open. Return the liquid to the clean pan and add the fish stock. Chop the remaining parsley finely and add it to the liquid with the chopped chilli. Bring to the boil, then lower the heat and simmer, stirring, for a few minutes until slightly reduced. Turn off the heat.

4 Remove and discard the top shells of about half the mussels and clams, reserving any juices. Put all the mussels and clams with their juices in the pan of liquid and season, then cover the pan tightly and set aside.

5 Cook the pasta in boiling salted water until al dente, i.e. just tender but still firm to the bite.

6 Drain the cooked pasta well, then return to the clean pan and toss with the remaining olive oil. Put the pan of shellfish over a high heat, toss to heat them through quickly and combine with the liquid and seasonings.

7 Divide the pasta among 4 or 6 warmed plates. Spoon the shellfish mixture over and then serve immediately, sprinkled with more parsley.